A Good Knight

a memoir of my arduous search for one good man

Robyn S. Brodie

StoriedLife
Publishing
Grand Haven, Michigan

ISBN 978-0692893999

Printed by CreateSpace, An Amazon.com Company.
Available from Amazon.com, CreateSpace.com, and other retail outlets.

Cover and book interior design:

Marie Kar – www.redframecreative.com

Cover images and photography credits:

Andrii Malysh ©123RF.com, ladyfortune ©123RF.com,
Ruethai Pramta ©123RF.com
© Face Photography / Shelley Tafelski

Website:

Storiedlifebyrobyn.com

to KJB

Contents

Prologue:
Good > Great

This is a collection of memories from my arduous search for a Knight. Notice I didn't even say a knight "in shining armor." Just a knight. Uh...well...maybe I should specify a little more: I was searching for a Good Knight. He didn't have to have all of the trappings of fairytales, like shiny chrome-colored armor and a perfectly white horse. On the contrary: his horse could be an appaloosa or a dappled grey. He would need a shield perhaps and a well-sharpened sword, but covered in head to toe in a coat of arms? Hah!

Why not you ask? Well, maybe you don't ask, but some have actually wondered why I would prefer a good knight instead of a GREAT knight, because it sounds like "settling." Here's why: because great knights only come in fairytales for the most part, where they are created greater than real. Perfectly white horses are not realistic either, nor even practical for that matter. And, a full coat of arms isn't available these days at a reasonable price, at least in my town.

All metaphorical kidding aside, fairytales do set us up for expectations as little kids, right?! Most of us fashion our idea of what the handsome prince or knight-in-shining armor will be like from reading and watching traditional princess stories, like Cinderella, Sleeping Beauty, and the Little Mermaid. I drew the line at Snow White however, because although her handsome prince fits the stereotype, to this day Snow White's singing voice makes my skin crawl right off my body. She sounds like she doesn't have a brain in her head.

But the other princess stories I grew up reading led me to believe that falling in love would be a fairytale with a magic ending, and that a great knight or handsome prince would arrive and sweep me up with a one-armed gesture mind you, onto the back of his horse as we rode off into the sunset. I would be in such a state of eternal blissful love that I of course would have no questions such as:

—Is there food and water where we're going?

—Will the little birds continue to bring me my bathrobe in the morning and sew a dress for me when I'd like something new?

—When I'm in a deep sleep or a bad mood, will my Great Knight's simple kiss wake and cheer me?

—Will my evil stepmother and stepsisters REALLY be out of my life for good?

—Could there be a pea under the mattress in my royal bedroom that could possibly ruin my sleep?

—Will I like the Knight's mother? If he's great, I'm SURE she'll be great, right?!

And so on and so on and so on.

Isn't it interesting that the princesses of fairytales never ask these questions? All said princess cared about was whether or not the shoe fit. If it did? Well, that's it then. She's getting married and moving to the castle. It's all perfect; the Knight is Great and that's enough.

And so I grew up on these ideals of love. I'll never forget my Grammy Brock and the first (and only) advice she gave me about relationships with men. She was married for 50 years after all and had seven children, so I figured she was entitled to an opinion. I was complaining to her one Thanksgiving about my boy problems in my parents' kitchen while she and I hovered over a pot of recently-drained, steaming russets. My complaint was regarding the dude-du-jour and his common insensitivities, how he should just know what to do and how to act in order for me to feel loved. I was twenty-five. Grammy Brock was eighty-four. There she was, all 105-pounds of her feisty, little perfectly-coiffed spunky propriety, and she looked at me and said:

"Well, it's really a shame if you have to tell him and lay it all out. But if you have to tell him? You have to tell him."

Period. Period meant period. That's it. No explanation, no elaboration from Grammy. I was therefore forced to take it at face value. Now, face value is hard for me 'cause I'm just a teensy weensy bit type-A and analytical. I tend to prefer the option of asking [at least] fifteen clarifying questions to make sure that it's safe to arrive at any conclusion. Yet, with one sentence, Grammy had popped the air out of my balloon: men are earthlings, not fairytale-lings. They are slightly clueless even when you meet the right one for you and you *will* spend your life telling him how to be sensitive to you and your needs. He. Will. Not. Just. Know.

Thanks a lot for the set-up, Disney!

If I were to be on an arduous journey for a Good Knight these days, I think my princess story would be more akin to the *Princess and the Frog* and honestly, I was thrilled when that movie came out. Here finally was a more realistic "fairytale," that the right guy may in fact seem like a frog at first and also that perhaps, even if you're a princess or would like to be one, you may have to adjust your expectations a bit. But I unfortunately did not have the benefit of a realistic princess story when I was little and impressionable. And it took me a while to learn what became my truth:

—A Knight can be a good, or a Knight can be great, but he
  can't be both.

Wait wait—don't slam my book shut! I can explain! Seriously, I realize it sounds pretty cut and dried, but ya see...*this* princess had gotten to the point in my desperation back then, where hard lines were necessary. I needed black and white specifications because smudging all of the colors into a purple-greyish hue had gotten me into trouble with my judgment. It is because of this that I needed to make the aforementioned my truth... so I would be able to discern what I wanted and needed, which was to find a Good Knight, not a great one. See, great knights have all of the trappings of romance and intrigue. I wanted to be scooped up and carried off into the sunset, remember? I had a proclivity for looking at one's accomplished feats and using it to solely define what "greatness" meant. I don't think this is an all-together inaccurate definition and I'll tell you why in a sec, but here is what you have to know at this very moment: I was raised on the Dutch work ethic, which at least here in West Michigan, pretty much means that a list of accomplishments is the [only] attribute that makes a person strong.

So, I therefore viewed greatness as having something to do with popularity and a vast-reaching influence. This view slowly grew, over the course of my young life, into a definition. And then? I took that definition, placed it in a tiny little box inside my heart and slapped a label on it in Sharpie-like fashion, that read: "The most reliable quality," when I was first looking for a knight. Interesting how my definition of "great" was reflective of the great knights in fairytales.

There's one person in particular I suspect had a little bit to do with my view-turned-definition. Allow me to introduce you to my Dad: now this man? This man was a great knight! He was so, to my young mind, given the greatness and vastness of his accomplishments; the entity of his established leadership was what I knew. Great knights built legacies, organizations, corporations and several 501c3's in their spare time for good measure. Great knights were intense and popular. They were out and about, involved and ambitious and didn't just have one horse and a castle; they had empires of respect around them.

Given my Dad's example, added to the other great knights he traveled in and among, I was looking for a man who was also known for a vast, intense, and popular standing in the community. Before I figured out I could take care of myself, I thought I needed all of that in order to be taken care OF. Ahhhhhh—would you suggest that I'd squarely made myself a distressed damsel? Yeh-huh, I did. My father never directly told me I should think this way. It was I who observed his unique gifts and capacities and deduced that when one is accomplished and therefore popular, it means they can take care of everybody else. I suspect my father would have preferred I took a lesson about self-reliance and independence from his example. Instead, I made the opposite conclusion. I pretty much strapped myself directly onto the train tracks, and I did this without realizing it for a very long time.

So choosing a person who was good over someone who maintained greatness may seem *like* taking less. But ohhhhhhh, not for this princess! In my case, embracing goodness over vastness was taking more for myself and my needs. It took a long time for me to figure out what I needed in a knight and what I came to learn about myself was that the word "good," as defined by me, Robyn Brodie, meant well-rounded, present, and whole. I needed a knight who had time. I needed a knight who wanted to spend time with *me* because he didn't use it all up conquering the world.

Now: world conquering is important—some worlds need to be conquered; therefore, some people are needed for the task of world conquering and that doesn't mean it's bad. It's just that my [eventual] personal preference was that a good knight be around a little more often than that, since world conquering is a full time job and all.

So yes, great feats are accomplished by great knights (and knightresses), but have you ever wondered why they aren't so good at maintaining their personal relationships? It's simple: there's not time for that! William Wallace, Abraham Lincoln, and JFK, didn't exactly have the most enriching relationships with their significant others. And do I really need to mention Bill and Hillary?

Ya see, I didn't realize that what I needed was a Good Knight until I was ribcage-deep into a seven-year relationship.

Yes, I said "seven."

Not only did I give away seven years, but it was a relationship marked by two broken engagements.

Yep. I said "two."

Twice engaged to the same un-prince. Nicely done, 'doncha think? It was only after the second broken engagement that I began to understand I'd wrongly labeled him a Good Knight.

He had seemed at first like a Knight-in-Shining-Armor. He was six years older. He was tall and dark and handsome and successful and noteworthy and accomplished. This was the surface attraction of fairytales and it was what I resonated with. I fell head-over-heels for this guy! I thought he was the one after the first sixty days of the whole seven-year ordeal. But by the time year two rolled around, the fairytale was wearing off and I began to see cracks in his armor. I'd found out he wasn't royalty after all. He had been nothing more than a commoner, which ironically I also was. Realizing his lack of royal status in addition to my own? This was not the most welcome news.

So, how could I stay with him for an additional...five...more...years?

Well, that is a great question, now isn't it?! I somehow thought this commoner needed a royal knight and I kept hanging onto the fairytale dream; I hoped he would buff his armor up. Oh, he had a pedigree all right—a business executive, a BMW, a bank account that could pay for nice dinners out and I fell for the image. I mean, let's be honest: what chick raised on fairytales wouldn't have been just a little bit hooked? In my youth, I wasn't disciplined enough to look past a facade to what was real underneath. Real seemed boring. Real seemed unfun.

I wanted to believe that what I thought I saw, was truly what was there.

So it wasn't until I was 32-years-old that I began the intentional search for a Good Knight. I didn't want a world conquerer anymore. I finally knew myself well enough to understand I wanted a guy who would go through each and every day *with* me. I wanted a "we"—not a him and a me in separate categories. That was what my parents were. I wanted more—I wanted oneness. I found out that I wasn't a damsel in distress and that shockingly, I didn't need to be rescued. I learned that I had the power to choose my own way out of cleaning cinders in the basement. If I no longer wanted to sleep in a cold, dirty attic? I actually did posses the key to open the creaky door and walk out of it by myself. Victims needed to be rescued. I was learning I wasn't one.

It left one problem though: I was thirty-two and running out of time. I wanted to have kids. So although this was an important epiphany to have finally absorbed, it was a little bit late and I was hearing a tick tock in my head. You know the one I'm talking about, Ladies.

What's a girl to do? Thirty-two wasn't exactly the ideal time for someone who wanted marriage and family in the traditional sense to begin looking...

Enter Bachelor Number One.

One: Drunk Church Boy

I was vibrant about my new boyfriend. He was charming and considering I had just dumped a big Lug of seven years, I had cause to be. After all, my biological clock was about to burst a spring any minute and here he had walked into my life with intent, fervor and a flirtation that said, "Me: Bee. You: Flower." I was not used to this kind of attention given the seven years of Cat & Mouse I'd played with the Lug (Him: cat. Me: Mouse). Combine the Cat & Mouse game with the Lug's dark persona and you get a relationship I called, the "Walking-Dead-Gerbil-Wheel" affair.

So after six weeks of seriously dating Burk [and by the way, when "Still Single at 32 in Michigan" is your identity, it doesn't take long to get serious], I was excited to take him to church with me on Thanksgiving weekend, which also happened to be my Mom's birthday. Here's why: I was pretty involved at my church; I was the lead vocalist on the music team, so had close friendships with leaders in all areas of programming. It was a smaller church (350 good-natured folks), yet dynamic and relational. But here's the thing: my church friends had standards for me and they didn't much care for The Lug. They thought I was settling, so I didn't bring him around much. One could deduce by this that I was leading a double life: praiseful on the weekends, yet dark and twisted during the weekdays with the Lug...but I'm getting a little ahead of myself.

So, given that my church family didn't care for the Lug, I assumed they would LOVE Burk. Get this people: Burk opened doors. Burk said "please" and "thank you." Burk made eye contact for goodness sake! Of course they would love him! And the truth is, I wanted their approval because I knew they were just looking out for me and I trusted them. This is Michigan and so, church here is a community of married couples with kids. I stood out like the kiwi garnish on a silver tray of bacon-wrapped-water-chestnuts. It wasn't codependence; it was a small group of trustworthy friends I considered mentors. I had asked for their opinion on the Lug and they had given me honest feedback.

So the night before the church introduction, Burk had spent the evening with one his old college buddies who happened to be in town, Mark Townsend; I was fine with catching up on things around the house since a new out-of-the-blue romance has a tendency to dominate one's spare time. I had weeks of laundry to do and thought I'd get a work out in. We planned that he would pick me up in the morning an hour before church, and then we'd make the 30-minute drive together. We talked at 7:30 that night—he and Mark sounded like they were having fun, yet Burk confessed that he "missed me." I did that cooing sound when I said, "Ooooh. I miss you toooooooo!" When we hung up, I reminisced about how lovely it was that Burk and I had a mature relationship, one that I could feel confident in even when we were apart. Ahhhhhh—just imagine doves flying out of a golden cage fluttering towards heaven, while Disney princess music plays, birdies chirp, and fawns lie about.

In the morning, Burk rolled his burgundy Ford Explorer into my driveway. I had been ready early, anticipating this big day of introducing Burk to my important friends and so saw him from my doorway. I walked out to meet him before he could get out. He hung his Scottish mop of red hair out of the car window wearing a sheepish grin. His hair did not look combed?! Okay...already? He is not meeting my expectations for this test he's about to take with the church people.

I walked closer to the car and then I smelled it: the brief stench of alcohol. I was already ticked before I got in the car searching for an alternative....ANY alternative, like maybe it was something the neighbor had perchance left out on the front porch? [A total reach because I hadn't even met my neighbor so didn't know if he/she was a drinker.] Please God, let it be the neighbor—not my perfect new boyfriend! I got in the car. He was still smiling sheepishly. I faked the "happy-to-see-you" smile. I refrained from kissing him, which is how we usually greeted each other.

He pulled out of the driveway and unfortunately, it didn't take long to realize that the alcohol stench was NOT from the neighbor's porch, nor was it "brief" as I'd ascertained a few minutes prior. Every time Burk spoke, I smelled it more. It was coming out of his pores. Burk smelled like a Scotch distillery. Suddenly, the doves were lame, the chirping birds were singing Taps, and the fawn? Well, now the fawn was a Bambi tragedy. I was *seething*. I. Could. Not. Believe. He. Would. Screw. Up. Something. So. Important?!

"Ahhh...Burk? You smell like you had a little bit too much to drink last night?!"

"I do??? Oh, yeh...well Mark and I finished off a fifth of Scotch. I guess we got a little carried away reminiscing about the good ol' days."

To myself: "Really Burk?? A *little*?" Even though I didn't say it out loud, he knew I was mad. In his defense, I don't think he had been clearly informed he was going to an audition for the part of "Robyn's Perfect Future Husband." But I still figured he would have had the good sense to not come semi-drunk to church.

We finally arrived and it was packed given the holiday weekend. My sister-in-law Jeannine had asked me to save her a seat since she was in the drama segment for the early part of the service. Since I had the morning off from singing, it was no problem. Jeannine was my best friend. She had already met Burk on several occasions and loved him, so thankfully I wasn't too nervous about her "impression." One down—349 to go.

So, Burk and I went and sat down in the theatre-style seated auditorium. It was elbow-to-elbow people and on my right was an empty seat I saved for Jeannine. Burk was seated on my left. Seated on his left? The assistant teaching pastor. I couldn't believe my luck. Why couldn't Burk have been seated next to another sinner with bad judgment??

Jeannine finished her segment and found her way to her saved seat. As the service moved along, I continued to smell that sour stench eminating from Burk. After a few moments, Jeannine leaned over towards me and while cupping her hand over my ear, she whispered, "This is really embarrassing but someone here really smells like alcohol!" I could have died.

I yelled back in the form of a whisper, "Yeh, I know. It's MY boyfriend!" Now she was stifling laughter: hand over the mouth... silently shaking...yet managing to whisper back, "It will be okay!" Somehow, I didn't share her hope. I was already thinking about my Mom's birthday and the event at my parents' house after the church service and how I had a long day to get through with Burk's unfortunate aroma.

After the service, we slowly walked out cattle-call style, like in a cinema when a popular movie has just finished and the credits are still rolling; it was slow goin'. It was all I could do not to have Burk greet the pastor he was seated next to. But being the friendly guy that Pete-the-Pastor was, he extended a hand and said, "You must be Robyn's new friend. Welcome!" I was behind Burk pulling on his coat as if to send him the telepathic message of "Don't open your mouth. You reek."

We finally escaped the herd and stopped at a wall in the back that was a little out of the way and Jeannine, knowing the perfectionist freak inside me was flipping out, went over to Burk and said nicely, intending helpfulness, "Hey Bud. I just want you to know that you really smell like alcohol. I'm only telling you so you don't lean in while shaking hands with people and go [as if to breathe fire out her mouth], 'HIIII! NIIIIICE TO MEEEEET YOU.'" Remember Jeannine was an actress? She played the part of the Drunk Church Boy perfectly.

Poor Burk. He muttered, "...Thanks...I think," sheepishly grinning again.

Jeannine, helpfully offered, "It's probably because you haven't eaten yet today. Once you do, it will mostly go away." Jeannine had tied one on a time or two, so she was an expert on such things. I wouldn't know as much because I was a wine girl. I drank wine *with* food. Apparently wine with food is a foreign concept?

After that, we went to Burger King and Burk ate a cheeseburger on the way to my Mom's birthday lunch. I was praying Jeannine was right about the food-alcohol-absorption theory. I don't even know to this day if my parents smelled Scotch on Burk at the birthday lunch (perhaps they smelled cheeseburger). I did know we made it out of church without running into any of my other VIP's. Whew!—There was a second chance for Burk to be perfect.

But what I came to learn is that when a person has the overall high qualities that Burk has, one screw-up even at the first meeting, isn't that big of a deal. Burk just made a mistake where I had created a circus full of hoops for him to jump through to make myself look good. My church family wasn't even putting that on me. I was putting it on myself. I set him up...I'd set myself up. Without me arranging it, Burk managed to eventually impress all of those same people on his own and without my help.

And I wish I could say the story had a happy ending right then and there, but unfortunately real life isn't usually like that. Remember I said this is what I "came to learn" ...meaning, over the course of time? Well, silly me got scared after that; I suspect this was because the Lug was a known commodity. Burk, although a great guy, was unknown so the idea of staying with him seemed farfetched. But I wasn't this self-aware back then. Back then, I needed to break up with Burk because he came drunk to church. Like, why would I put up with this same kind of disrespectful and immature treatment when I could get it with the one that also brought the comfort of familiarity? 'Seemed like evaluative logic at the time. So, I broke up with Burk and ended up back with the Lug (...as if the one incident of Burk's insensitivity was equal to seven years of it from the Lug). Lug was a person who was willing to move heaven and earth to get what he wanted but wouldn't lift a finger to keep it.

So, once again Cat & Mouse wooed me back to the dysfunction of itself right before Christmas, considering Lug's bribery technique of enticing lavish gifts and promises of "I'll change this time,"... and Burk? He went home to Massachusetts to see his folks and nurse his broken heart. Can you imagine having the scenario, "If only I hadn't gone semi-drunk to church, she'd still be dating me" play through your head on Christmas? Ay yi yi.

But in true Lug-like fashion, Lug and I ended things a few months later and I felt like a used up dirty dishrag.

So the moral of the story [and for the record, I'm not usually into moral pronouncements in/on "stories" because we literature snobs feel story "morals" to be a little base for our dignified analysis levels. I mean, we can figure out the moral on our own thank you very much, without an overt explanation! But since this actually happened and isn't fiction for the sake of analysis, I'm making an exception... you're welcome.]

Ahem...where was I...Oh yeh: the moral of the story, my friends, is really a *question*: how much of what I want and need, or *think* I want and need is truly dictated by the expectations of others? Or, how much of it is self-inflicted by my own lack of self-worth? For me, it was more about the latter than I could see at the time! Who cares if I was 32, unmarried, and with a uterus that was wasting away?! Even *if* everyone here in West Michigan thought it was weird that I was still single, it didn't matter. My life had worth regardless. And in truth? I was the one who thought I was weird for not having the Grade-A-Marriage Stamp on my life, not the church people. Not any people.

Well, except for the old aunts at holiday gatherings who didn't have a file for remaining single past the age of 22, let alone 32. My Mom had four sisters and they were the guilty culprits of a portion of my neurosis. Of the four aunts, three were divorced, so it did beg the question, "Uhhhh perhaps if YOU'D waited Ladies, ...taken a little more time in shopping for a Good Knight, you would have chosen better men and thus still be married??"

Yet, they couldn't help pointing out the obvious: one time at a Christmas gathering at my Aunt Bonnie's house (who by the way is the most beautiful creature I've perhaps ever seen), she greeted me with, "Oh my dearest Robyn, you're still ah...ah...alone?" Nice. Next Aunt Lulu said to me at the same gathering, while holding a punch cup in one hand and a plate of nuts in the other, "Hi Robyn. No husband yet?" What did people think? Did they *think* I enjoyed the awkwardness of my singleness? Did they think I liked being the bridesmaid standing next to the twelve-year-olds in the bouquet toss at wedding receptions where I was always the bridesmaid? Because it's such a blast to be *that girl*? I won't tell you what my Aunt Dolly said because she was wearing two shoes that didn't match and had caked liquid-eyeliner on only one of her eyes—Aunt Dolly wasn't quite all together there I don't think, so her comments dripped off me in a way the others' didn't.

It wasn't just the aunts though—it was also some of my Mom's friends, Edna and Beatrice, who said things like, "Poor Robyn—she just can't seem to meet a nice guy" and "at this rate, she'll probably never have babies." It didn't help that my own mother (who to this day is mind-numbingly blunt) said, "Robyn, you know, …people say that you are an…'enigma.'"

"Enig-whut Mother??"

"Enigma. Because you're so pretty and talented and yet…you just can't find that *one*." This is the same woman who when a good friend of mine had a baby said, "That's the ugliest baby I've ever seen." She said it loud enough that others could have heard her. And another time we were at Meijer, and she said, "I don't know why people let themselves get so fat?" Out loud. In public. At the Meijer. Within earshot of a weight-challenged person. To this day her lack of political correctness astounds me: she still says "Hyper-kinesis" to describe ADHD, she says "black" instead of African American and says "retarded" to describe someone who has learning disabilities or mental challenges. Now: my Mom had a special-needs child of her own, my older brother. So, she had NO intention of ever being hurtful. She just didn't change with the times in her language. However, as much as I adore my mother, it's no wonder that she would find the insulting of my singleness identity a "light" topic. At least in her opinion I wasn't "ugly" like the baby or "fat" like the shopper. I just wasn't a good husband finder.

So, it's not as if my own family made it easy on me to remain untroubled about my self-worth. But outside of them, there weren't a lot of people who thought I was weird. I wasn't weird to the world at large. I was just weird to myself. And because of it, I'd even reasoned at one point that marrying the wrong man was better than no man. Can you imagine choosing to be eternally unhappy just because of the way you falsely believed the world at large defined you? I almost did that.

Regardless of the aunts though or anyone else, the more I believed what was actually true about me, the less the actions or inactions of others mattered. What was actually true was that I needed a Good Knight, not a great one, and he was worth waiting for no matter how long it took.

Two: How Did I Get Here?
(a.k.a. The Castro, Cokie and a Ferrari)

There is a reoccurring theme in my life that makes me wonder how I end up in places. I'll explain more later as to why it befuddles me, but let me just tell you that accidentally ending up in the Castro once is not the first inadvertent, geographical positioning I've experienced, nor was it the last. When I was dating the Lug, he took me to San Francisco a couple of times to visit his brother. Lug owned some stock in a small travel agency and was able to procure travel deals from time to time. [Thank goodness Lug had *some* advantages, right? Of the few, this was one.]

I'd actually been to San Francisco once before when I was a kid given my father's propensity to combine business trips with family vacations. A Dutch man never misses a chance to take a tax write-off while convincing his family this "family vacation" would be "a blast." You laugh? Well, I've taken many a tour through meat packing plants in my day, [Granger Colorado not withstanding] seeing whole carcasses of steer hanging from the ceiling in infinite rows while hearing the sounds of butchering from somewhere out back. So the San Francisco family trip was the best of them for sure, Mom taking us to Ghirardelli Square and Fisherman's Wharf while Dad went to meetings. [And I can say that about my penny-pinching-Dutch Dad, because he passed it onto me. Here's what they say in this neck of the woods: How do you start a parade in West Michigan? Roll a penny down the street.]

Anywho, when Lug wanted to go visit his brother, I was excited to go again because I knew how gorgeous it was there. I'd seen the Golden Gate Bridge before after all! We stayed with his brother Sean and Sean's fiancée, Brooke. Sean was an investment banker and Brooke an interior designer.

The first night we were there, Brooke asked, "Since Lug and Sean are going hand gliding tomorrow, do you want to go with me to my hair appointment?"

"Sure," I said, thinking it was cool to hang out with her no matter what we were doing. Brooke was a fascinating person, smart and sophisticated. Of course, I tried to shield what I thought she may perceive as my Midwest small-town naiveté, which for the most part I'd done a pretty good job of concealing, up until a point.

Here's when the point occurred: the next day as the guys went off to fly around, Brooke and I went to her hair appointment. We hopped in her Jeep, top and sides off, and drove over the Golden Gate Bridge to Marin County in the gorgeous spring air. It took awhile to get where we were going.

Finally, Brooke said, "Just so you know, I go to the Castro to get my hair done. It's so much cheaper there than in my neighborhood, and the gay guys do a way better job."

"Yeh, 'the Castro' is the gay neighborhood, right?" (I faked that I already knew what the Castro was. I knew that San Fran had "the highest number of homosexuals per capita than any other city in the United States," because I had learned it in college, but that's really all I knew.)

"Yes, the gay neighborhood." Then Brooke went onto explain what I had not learned in college, which was that most of them congregated in one neighborhood because historically going back to World War II, even in seemingly progressive San Fran, there had been little social tolerance for homosexuals and that it was more comfortable for them to have their own community. Alrighty then. I am up to speed!

So, we arrived at the salon Brooke frequented. I went in with her, and I will tell you, these were some funky looking dudes. They had facial piercings, mohawks, AND tattoos. [...remember, ...this was Robyn circa '93]. They didn't look like Rock Hudson that I'd seen tattered across the pages of the National Inquirer. Apparently there was more to know than inquiring minds had previously demanded.

"You don't have to hang out in here Rob. You can go walk around if you'd like while I sit here," Julie offered. Good idea.

"I'll be back in a half an hour or so," and off I went to explore the neighborhood. Well, let me just tell you that this chickie from the Midwest got more than an eyeful of information and an education on what being gay *could* mean. It was the first time in my life I realized I'd been sheltered. I saw biker chicks with shaved heads, spiked collars (like a bulldog) and eyebrow piercings, all on the same chick. I saw girlie men making out (bumping and grinding actually) on the street corner, and transvestites/cross-dressers blowing kisses at each other on a park bench.

I walked by a shop that had sex toys in the window for sale, that I wasn't even sure which sexual act they were used for. I tried to reason out what they were, I really did. I still didn't know. Can I ask: what happened to the "discreet brown package" that could be delivered safely to a customer's door without anyone else's knowledge? Apparently, community members of The Castro were sick of hiding. I don't blame them. I mean, I'm still enough-uvva-goody-two-shoes to think that something resembling a dildo should not be displayed for sale in the front window of a shop at a child's eye level, but that's what happens when society harshly judges people: the pendulum shifts too far the other direction. The Castro definitely had a "take-THAT, you-smug-Hetro" kind of attitude about it, and, although I didn't necessarily like it, I did sort of understand it.

But here's the point anyway: the question struck me, how did I get here? What's a little blonde from Michigan doing in this neighborhood? I'm clearly clueless and stand out like a pimple on a Homecoming Queen's nose. (...maybe there's a chance the chicks and dudes here will think I'm like Brooke, who came to take advantage of the perfectly reasonable hairstyling prices?) And besides, I had gay acquaintances; in fact, my own stylist back home was gay! And I had been places: I'd seen the Statue of Liberty and Niagara Falls for crying out loud (even if it was on a wholesale-food-business trip). I'd even, a couple of years back, performed professional vocals for a musical event in Manila, the Philippines and had been to Hong Kong. (Haven't you seen everything once you've been to Hong Kong? I offer this as a fair argument. If you've ever been there, you know what I mean.)

But here I stood, in the middle of the Castro imagining a camera zooming out from a crane shot of me that made me look (without needing words to describe it), like the truest fish out of water that had ever accidentally ended up on dry land. It was crazy: all 110 pounds of impressionable naiveté' complete with well...big hair, and NO spikes or tattoos, along with a side of cluelessness to complete the look. How did I get here?

When I met back up with Brooke, she asked me what I thought. Not wanting to stand out as uninformed as I was, I responded that, "it was cool." I figured she might be secretly laughing because she perceived I was clueless, which is why she suggested I go for a walk in the first place. I thought I had reasonably acted my way out of appearing inexperienced but well, I'm pretty sure she didn't buy it. In fact, this was a woman who eventually got married at the San Francisco Art Museum and who decorated the swankiest new hot-spot restaurant in town. I know she didn't buy it!

But it seems I have a life pattern of ending up in places or situations where I am forced to ask myself, "how did I get here?" It affects me as incredulous because as I've mentioned, I am a box-checking perfectionist. I only need to learn the hard way once, and I learn for life. I think ahead about everything, from what if it might rain today (better have a coat in the backseat just in case)—to better not travel on spring break with the other families because we have an increased risk of getting stuck somewhere in an airport then—to always remembering to pack Pepto-Bismol on an overnighter because you just never know! Let's just say my planning has come in handy on several occasions. But because of it, I am then shocked when things don't go *as planned* and I find myself somehow standing in the middle of the Castro.

Jeannine, for example, is the opposite from me. Jeannine doesn't plan ahead for anything. In fact, if you ask Jeannine "what's for dinner" as late as 5:00 pm, she will snarl at you. She doesn't make plans. She doesn't make reservations at restaurants (she is surprised to find out that at 2 o'clock on New Year's Eve afternoon, her favorite spot is "all booked up" for that night.) In Jeannine's defense however, she happily lives with the consequences. Jeannine would not pack Pepto-Bismol, would phlegmatically travel via airplanes/airports on Spring Break, and will wait 90 minutes to be seated for a meal at a restaurant even though the fallout from not planning for these situations dictates waiting, hunger pangs, boredom and diarrhea. She doesn't care. So who am I to say everyone should be an uptight planner like me? The point is, Jeannine rarely, if ever, has to ask herself "How did I get here?" because she knows on any given day she could end up in some funky situation. Jeannine wouldn't be surprised that she ended up in the Castro by accident, even if she started the day in Michigan with no travel plans.

So as I mentioned, the theme-question, how did I get here, has happened to me on many occasions. The Castro does stand out I think because of the magnitude of my credulity—still, I have questions about how someone as constrained by my own effort to control risk (like thinking to pack Pepto) can not avert the destiny that must be sometimes. Fate will find its way to just be.

Along these lines, there was the time I ended up having lunch with Cokie Roberts, accidentally of course. I knew that I was invited to an event called "January Series" at Calvin College. I knew that I was not the technical invitee' exactly, but the guest of the person who was. I knew that there was a seminar where Cokie would speak to a group of about a thousand and I knew I was going to a meeting with my date afterwards, where lunch would be served and that the president of the college would also be at this lunch—it sounded like your classic academic banquet-room luncheon.

These were all plan-able plans. I knew what to wear, I knew how to act, I knew what I needed to bring in my purse (Pepto probably not needed since it was a few only hours of time) and I knew I needed to listen a lot, not talk too much—because my date was the contact person. So I went in my appropriate black suit and professional hairstyle and dialed-back repartee. Once there and after Cokie gave her dynamic speech, we walked to....the President's house! This lunch was at the President's....*house*? Not only that, but there were only twenty people at the lunch! And oh yeh, Cokie Roberts was one of the twenty and I was one of the twenty and the President of the college was also one of the twenty. My date did not prepare me for this experience. I was absolutely thrilled but also absolutely caught off guard especially because I was seated kitty-corner from the college president, and two down from Cokie. Cokie Roberts: I still can't believe that happened to me—you might be thinking, "big freakin' whup Brodie—it wasn't Brad Pitt, George Clooney, Justin Bieber or Lady Gaga or the President of the United States or Derek Jeeter or Madonna or Jennifer Lopez or Rachael Ray or Ryan Gosling or Miley Cyrus or Kobe Bryant or Michael Phelps or any number of people. But for a writer?? To sit two down from a New York Times best selling author? To chat like we were friends with a national journalist whose been seen on hard-news television every week for 20 years? Big effin' deal for me people, big effing deal!!

How did that happen to me? How did I get here? I'm just a little person with a simple, private life from Grand Haven, Michigan. How did I end up at *this lunch* chatting with Cokie? And it really was a riot because, out of the remaining sixteen attendees minus Cokie, the pres, my date and myself, the rest of them were all presidents of the local TV stations in Grand Rapids, the President of NPR radio Michigan, the senior editor of Baker Publishing Company and on and on. And me.

Another time, a date and I were headed to St. Louis to visit friends. We stopped off in Chicago for a night to break up the trip. I had asked my brother Cole, to call one of his friends who lived there for a restaurant recommendation, because there's always something new and exciting in Chicago when it comes to culinary mastery. SO, I texted Cole and this is exactly what I said: "We want 'hip,' NOT hoity-toity."

Cole texted back a couple of hours later and said, "My friend Brad said to go to 'Blackbird on Rush Street.'" Okay! So we made a reservation at Blackbird and were looking forward to it, after having left town around 3:00 pm Michigan time. Chicago is an hour behind so at about six pm, CST, we walked into Blackbird. The host looked so far down his nose, I swear he focused in on a clogged pore on the tip of it. We were ushered to a table and there wasn't one thing on the the menu that I recognized! It was the first time I'd ever heard of "Monkfish." What's monkfish? A swimming monkey?

As the food came, it was all a surprise because the server felt that we should "just know" what the words on the menu meant and was put off by our inquiries. As each plate was presented, we noticed a morsel of food in the middle of an enormous round dish that looked like the speck on Horton's trunk. The plates had smears of green and orange down the side. It was clearly food art, which is fine if that's what you want but we didn't—we wanted energy, fun, and hip. Instead, we got stuck up, non-communicative and frankly at the end of the night? Hunger! Dinner was $125 dollars and after all that, we wanted to stop off for a sandwich before calling it a night!

To add insult to the already-injured nature of the snob-effect, on the back of the menu it read, "Suits by Hugo Boss." Okay, I ask you: how many restaurants have you been to where the servers wear designer business suits? (Isn't that a little dangerous? What if they spill something on that two-thousand-dollar sharkskin? Serving is a high risk for spillage occupation.) But after awhile, it just got funny. So nearing the end of the meal when the server presented us with our dessert options, in spite of the fact that we hadn't asked to see a dessert menu mind you, we decided to have a little fun with him. He ran through a litany of gourmet pastryish foods—he mentioned something about "ciafouti" and "chickory crumble" and then without smiling, he looked at us and asked (in the Ferris Bueller-Ben-Stein voice): "Which would be your preference?" He was correct in assuming we had room for dessert since the portion sizes had been minuscule, but we again did not recognize the name of the options, so I said, fighting back a laugh, "Do...you...have anything that resembles chocolate cake?"

"No." Affirmative.

We stared at him incredulously, like how dare you not have chocolate cake?! He finally became uncomfortable with the silence and our stares, and yet again in that Ben Stein Bueller voice said: "I think...I may...have a ...cookie."

Ohhhhhkay then. Let's go with a cookie, shall we?

We had taken note of the very supposedly wealthy patrons around us, who if were not high-society types, were doing a pretty good job pretending. But it was only as we were leaving I figured out that they were for real, because parked outside on the curb right in front of the restaurant was a Ferrari! A *red* Ferrari, and the paint was so shiny, I could see my reflection. As the dweeb I am, I insisted on taking a picture with my cell phone (which was a "thing" back in the flip-phone-non-smart era). Yet again I asked: what am I doing here? A few hours ago, shortly before 3 pm Michigan time, while babysitting, I was scraping poop off a baby's butt and finishing up a grad school paper. Yet, now I'm here...at a restaurant that celebrities and the wealthy frequent...and there is a FERRARI parked outside! How did I end up *here?* I actually tried to go back inside to try to play a little game—it was a new game I called, "The Let's-See-Whose-Car-We-Think-This-Is" game. My date wasn't into it, so I let it go. I'm just sayin' though, it's not something I see everyday!

So even when I try to plan for events, probables or the likelihood of what's expected, often the unexpected happens and it always fascinates me. I planned to go to San Francisco (I mean, it's a BIG city), not the Castro specifically, but there I was anyway. I planned to go to a seminar-lunch-type-thing at Calvin College, but I had lunch at the President's house with Cokie. And I planned to go to a hip energetic restaurant in Chicago, but ended up in a luxurious eatery, sitting next to someone who drives a Ferrari. I am a planner. I plan and plan and plan and plan. And when things don't go as planned, I'm either irritated or fascinated.

So, how did I end up here on an arduous search for a Good Knight at the age of 32? All together now: [Please figuratively imagine it as I raise my arms as if to direct a choir,]...Because, THINGS DIDN'T GO AS PLANNED.

Good job. Way to work together as a group on that anthem!

Three: I'll Tell You How I Got Here!

So, the Castro experience (and ending up there by accident) really DID happen to me, but I am including it for one reason: it's a metaphor. Wow.....you're really glad I took the time to point that out, right?? I should have used a bigger build up, like an extensive drum roll followed by a cymbal bash. But I digress.

Given the question of, how did I get to the point where I was willing to date so many, many colorful characters? [...which, calling them "colorful" is being generous to most of them...just sayin'...] Here's how: as I mentioned, being single past the age of thirty in a Midwestern beach town is an accomplishment—even those who try to remain single can't do it. Everything is done in pairs and families here. Ya know when you're feeling pudgy and want to lose weight and wherever you look there seems to be a skinny girl? Well, being single around here and wanting to be married causes consistent sightings of young couples kissing every time you go the beach or an elderly couple walking through the park holding hands. It was nauseating. Suffice it to say, it's difficult to be a party of one. So one day, I was complaining about my "situation" to the counseling pastor at church and he said: "Hmmmmp. Ya know what Robyn? I am going to put you in touch with my twin sister Penny! Penny didn't get married 'til she was 36! She had her babies at 38 and 40!" [It was as if he were a game-show host getting ready to show me what was behind door number three.] Don't get me wrong: ol' Kenny was being completely sincere, but I had been going on about this woeful situation of singleness that I had been dealing with for quite some time, so I think even *he* was excited to show me what was behind door number three.

So, I talked to Penny on the phone the next week and here's what she said: "Stop being lonely. You're an attractive girl—if you put out vibes like you'll go out with people, you'll get asked out. Go out with whomever asks."

"Whut?? Whom*ever*?"

"Yeh. And not only that, tell your friends that you're open to meeting someone."

"But what about 'The Lug?' "

"At some point you know, you have to cut him loose in your mind— you're not even dating him anymore and you know it's the right decision after all you've told me, but you have to cut it off in your heart."

"I know...I know."

"Here's the thing Robyn: you can stay home and be lonely but you won't meet a spouse that way. Go out with anyone and everyone. If they're willing to buy you dinner on Friday night, why are you staying home? What are you afraid of?" So I rolled this unconventional advice around in my head for a few days, what she had said about going out with "whomever asked" and realized she was right: "he" wasn't showing up at my door and so I took her advice. THAT's how I got here.

And so it began. I began dating every Tom, Dick, and Harry that slithered by. To be fair, some of them didn't slither: some of them actually stood erect, some of them swam (bottom feeders) and some of them inched along like a caterpillars. Finding a Good Knight would be no small task.

Pause: why couldn't it happen like the way Jeannine met my brother, at a gas station in Indiana? Ya walk into a gas station one day and you meet your husband. That's it—that's how they met. (Although... Jeannine would be mad at me if I weren't honest about the fact that she dated every Tom, Dick, and Harry too before she met my brother.) But at least she didn't have to sit in her house and put out an all-points bulletin: "Hello. Yes, it's me Robyn. I am in the market for a husband. Do you know any single men??" I made that phone call thirteen times in one day. I seriously did that.

But guess what? It was effective. So the inchers, slitherers and slatherers, along with the few humans who stood erect, began calling, and I actually began kind of enjoying the fact that I was "on the market." Line 'em up. Rack 'em up—it was definitely a parade. Committed to no one—serious with no one—paying for little to nothing—and occasionally biting my lip not to laugh at some of the people I ended up across a dinner table from.

It was true that I still [on occasion] pined for The Lug. But it was mostly because he was what I knew—Lug was familiar—he was a known entity. Everyone else, Burk included, were foreign to me. In the past, I'd always reached back for the familiar, even when it was bad because I figured it was less scary and threatening than what might be better. So, I was certainly feeling strange about it all, but at the same time, I didn't miss the Lug as much as I thought I would.

Four:
Car-Lose and Love-notes

Allow me to introduce you to Carlos. Carlos had come to my church with a friend and had apparently seen me sing at one of the services. After church, he had his friend pass me a note, which I didn't have time to read in the moment because I was racing out. Having not met Carlos, I thought it was "romantic" that there was a little white piece of paper in the lining of my bag just waiting for me to drink in its message. So, I saved it for just such a special moment, where I could give it my undivided attention.

When I got home, I crawled up on my bed, crossed my legs and took a deep breath, giving the note the proper respect it deserved with a moment of silence, like the yoga-OM pose. Then I read it:

Dear Robyn,

I saw you sing in church today and I was so taken with you. You seem to love what you're doing. Your facial expressions were exquisite and your smile warmed my heart. Here is my phone number if you'd like to meet for coffee or a meal.

All my admiration,
Carlos

My first thought: I am so flattered.

My second thought: I am cheesed out.

My third thought: Really Penny? Everybody? I'm suppose to go out with everybody who asks? Did you see that line about my "facial expressions," Penny? Did you? Did you? Huh???

Big sigh: this one could have been easy to refuse because after all, he gave me his phone number and asked me to call *him*, so it would have been fine to let him think I didn't get his note or wasn't interested.

Sidebar: In defense of Carlos and on the topic of cheesy notes, I had to admit that his note wasn't the cheesiest "love" note I'd ever received in my life: in the sixth grade a boy named Ronny Heorle [pronounced, "hurl," as in "hurl chunks"], passed me a note in Sunday school scrawled on a Hershey Bar wrapper that said and I kid you not:

> *My heart is throbbin' for Robyn*
>
> *My love is gobbin' for Robyn*

Wait, there's more!

> *I am SOBBIN' for Robyn*

Even my eleven-year-old sixth grade heart knew this was cheesy. So, Love-notes and I had a past; I had a connotation with them as you will, a connotation that screamed, "RUN! Run as fast and far away as you can!"

But...deep breath: I was 32. I wanted to get married and I wanted to have kids. I ran Penny's remarks back through my mind. She was right, he wasn't going to show up at my door. He was out there. I hadn't met Carlos. I didn't know what he looked like. His note *was* cheesy to say the least. But I knew I had to give it a shot. What did I have to lose except for another ovulating egg? If I remained this vigilantly picky, I would eventually run out of eggs.

Therefore, I called Carlos. He sounded pleasant and less cheesy in his spoken word versus his written one. So on that Sunday night, we made plans to go out for the next Friday night. I admittedly looked forward to it all week. He insisted on picking me up—I didn't want to do it that way, yet I could sense he was trying to be chivalrous. It had been a long time since I'd been out with a true gentleman, so his appeal won me over.

Here's is how the date went after my bold, yet thoughtful decision to allow him to pick me up:

He was actually as pleasant in person as he had sounded on the phone and was indeed a gentleman. But!...he drove slower than a cherry picker on the Dan Ryan. And we drove slowly ALLLLLLLLL the waaaaaaaaaay to Grand Rapids—which? Should normally take thirty-five minutes. But it took an HOUR. The slow driving echoed the awkwardness of our slow conversation. I kept trying to spin the conversation into new topics in spite of the fact that he was going fifty-five in a seventy mile per hour zone! For the record, I am a fast chick: I walk fast. I talk fast. I write fast. I type fast. I dial the phone fast. I make lunch fast, and I admittedly...probably...umm...drive fast. I'm not suggesting that he should have been speeding. But what I cannot take is when someone isn't, at the very least, driving the speed limit! Jee-yimity!

Trying to avoid the urge to find a serrated edged-object to plunge into my own chest due to the snail-like nature of his driving, I tried again with the conversation. It went something like this:

"So Carlos... do you like...err...sunsets?" I pulled it out of my butt in an act of desperation as to not die of complete and utter boredom. I acted like "sunsets" was a topic that, of course, everyone discusses on the first date, pretending that, "Do you like....sunsets" is the same type of ice-breaker question as, "What do you do for a living?" Seriously, 'sunsets' for crying out loud? Could I be more lame in my attempt at self-rescue?

"Yeh I like sunsets." Crickets. [Would you care to elaborate on that Carlos, like...you saw the prettiest sunset one time at

_____? Nope. Carlos would not care to elaborate.]
fill in the blank

"What do you do for fun?" ['Doing better at pulling a less random topic out of my butt.]

"I play in a baseball league in Holland." Again, awkward silence.

Alrighty then. So I decided to let him feel the silence and stopped asking questions. It was uncomfortably silent until he casually mentioned that he was divorced and had FOUR kids. Okay: I had long given up the idea that I would find a Good Knight who had not yet had children. Men within a five year radius of my age on either side had kids. It wasn't my first choice to marry into an already-established family, but I knew that the odds of finding Mr. Right without being willing to, were very small. But four children? Their ages spread out from three to thirteen. Four kids and an ex-wife (maybe more than one ex??) I'm not feelin' the love Carlos—I'm just not feelin' it and I'm on my way TO Grand Rapids...in your car...going turtle speed...and I already know I'd never call you again. I heaved an enormous internal sigh of relief when we fin-al-ly reached the restaurant in downtown Grand Rapids.

So you can imagine how the rest of the evening dragged along. Carlos chose a tapas place called "San Chez." I was pleased when we pulled up because he hadn't told me where we were going in order for it to remain a surprise. And Oh, I was REALLY on the edge of my seat with anticipation at this point 'doncha know?! So thankfully after all that, it turned out to be a place I'd heard of and had been meaning to try.

San Chez was really nice and the food was great, but it wasn't over-the-top expensive or anything. Yet, at the end of the dinner, the check came and he picked it up and looked at it; then he looked up from the check and straight at me and said this: "Okay. I'll get it this time, but next time, we'll go Dutch, okay?"

I blinked like a cartoon character.

I'm not sure what I said out loud but it must have been "okay" because he flashed this enormous smile at me and I was absolutely astounded. I don't remember walking out of the restaurant or walking to the car. Ladies, can I get a witness? He said I had "beautiful facial expressions" for crying out loud?! He said my smile "warmed his heart." Would one not also assume then, that he was paying for dinner??

So at this point, I'd imagine you are thinking I asked him to take me home. Well...let me tell ya—I wasn't very good at setting boundaries back then (clearly not, since I had given much of my child-bearing years to the Lug, even though he treated me poorly). I was way too worried about what people thought. As if I had something to lose with Carlos if I'd ended the date right then and there (AFTER the three-hour drive it would take to get back to my house.) But NOOOOOOOOOOOOOOOOOO! Could I say NO to the rest of the evening? Uvvvve course I couldn't!!

So he asked if I would like to get a movie. He said, "I have a nice house in Holland and two roommates," indicating that it was a safe-enough atmosphere. I said "sure," instead of "take me home, I never want to see you again."

Once arriving at his house with the movie, we went down to his "bedroom" to watch it, which was really the unfinished basement of the house where his bed was next to the laundry machine. Oh, he was right about the house being nice alright....except the part he lived in. There was a sheet on a clothesline separating his "room" from the remainder of the basement. I know this sounds scary and creepy but he was harmless—the scene was just hilarious because we had traveled a toilsome pilgrimage from my lovely facial expressions to this basement with a cracked cement floor. There I stood in my cute little outfit trying not to laugh at the fact that he REALLY believed he was doing all of the right things to impress me!

So, he said, "wait here," while he skipped over to his bed and pushed it against the wall in order to make it a "couch" so we could then lean up against the cement wall while we watched the movie on his 7-inch screen TV. His TV was seriously smaller than a box of Cheeze-Its. His bed, having been moved, revealed a plethora of shoes and boxes and even a soccer ball rolled freely in the open area now that the bed was a "sofa."

The movie was great actually, so I gave him a chicken scratch in the other column for that. He had chosen *Selena* starring Jennifer Lopez and I thought I was in for another bad, slow experience, but thank goodness it was actually entertaining! Yet the entire time, he never even offered me so much as a glass of water.

That night while I was taking off my make-up, I looked in the mirror and thought I had to be the unluckiest girl in the world and that Penny could go to hell along with her advice. I confessed my sins the next morning, but I really couldn't believe I had given up six hours of my life for that.

And I will have you know that it was the very last time I ever let a date pick me up at my house.

Five:
And Then There Was Nate

And then there was Nate. Nate Peterson. I'm not exactly sure how I met him. Pretty great for a memoir, huh, that I don't re-mem-ber how I met him. But it's true. And I guess that tells you something about the impression he made too. But hey, I'm getting ahead of myself. Nate was actually pretty fantastic at first, unlike Carlos. I actually wanted Nate to call me again after our first date...and then again after our second date. But by about the third date (or it could have even been the fourth 'cause he *was* cute), I was beginning to feel hesitant towards him.

One night, I was sitting cross-legged again [no yoga pose this time though...] on my couch with a pillow in my lap and a laptop on top, typing my English homework. This was a hard position to get myself into and out of, but I liked writing that way—it made me feel comforted in that nook of the sofa, so I'd learned to keep the phone on the arm rest. When Nate called I was willing to answer because although I wasn't crazy about him, I'd had fun with Nate and wanted to find out where it could go.

"Hello?"

"Hi Beautiful!"

"Hey there Nate."

"So, you know that couple I talk about all of the time, Jeff and Tonya?"

"Yeh..."

"Well....I want you to meet them! What are you doing tomorrow night? Can you come to Grand Rapids? We want to go to the FishHouse at The BOB!" Hmmmm. Dinner out with friends. I knew I shouldn't go because I had a mountain of homework and it wasn't a night I drove into Grand Rapids anyway, so I was hesitant. See, Nate and I had met for wine after the start of the Griffins' games. I'd drive into Grand Rapids, sing the National Anthem for the Griffins' game (an IHL hockey team), get paid thirty dollars, and then walk across the street to the wine bar where I'd spent it on wine with Nate.

Now, I know how this looks—it looks like I'm paying but really, I was intentionally paying for myself so he didn't get the wrong idea. I was interested in him but not ready for him to be my boyfriend. I was taking Penny's advice: "Don't sit home—go out with everyone and anyone." But I'd found on occasion, that letting men pay meant they expected a commitment of either mind, body or soul. Some expected all three after one dinner. Not happening. So paying for myself on occasion was healthy!

But...on one of those wine dates, I'd found out that Nate lived at home with his parents. Hmmmmm. Now: I was patient about that because there had been a recent time where I'd sold a business on which I'd taken a financial loss, and had needed to move back in with my parents for a year. I was of course anxious to get out, so I worked my butt off to be able to afford to get out and did as soon as I could. I didn't know enough about Nate yet to understand whether he was comfortable at home with his parents or in the same boat I'd been in, so I reserved judgment. The only thing I knew was that he did have a good job. Yet, this invitation to a high-end restaurant where he would pay sounded like an official date. He was introducing me to friends too, so I figured I was about to find out if he'd "...get this one but the next time we'll go Dutch," OR, if it was for real.

"Well...I'm not going to be downtown tomorrow night anyway," I told him, "but...let me see if I can work it out." I hung up in order to give myself a chance to think about it, promising to call him back "in a few." I took a break from paraphrasing poetry. [By the way, as a teacher, I do understand that paraphrasing is essential, in order to learn how to pull the deeper meaning out of difficult poems...'cause poems are hard and we need tools], but paraphrasing "*The Little Red Wheelbarrow*," by William Carlos Williams? Here: let me show you what I mean. What can you make from this, even if you put it your own words:

so much depends
upon

a red wheel
barrow

glazed with rain
water

beside the white
chickens.

Just sayin'. I guess I needed a break from William. So, I pieced together my plot for going to the FishHouse and called Nate back and accepted his invite.

We met up prior to the date the next evening in the doorway of the Big Old Building downtown where the FishHouse was. Nate looked handsome in a green dress shirt. He was smiling the "Ahhhhh—there she is" smile. I greeted him and he introduced me to his friends, Jeff and Tonya. Once we all sat down at the table, I began looking over the FishHouse menu. Okay, here's the thing, People: I don't like fish. Never have. When anyone insists I should try this one or that one because it doesn't taste "fishy like other fish" I always taste the fishy. I do like shellfish, but there isn't one actual fish (without a shell) I've ever tasted that I've liked! I'll eat it for the sake of good manners, like for example, if I accepted a dinner invitation to someone else's home—then I'd eat what has been provided for me. 'Just like my Mom taught me, "One bite to be polite." But, if presented with a *choice*, I'll always choose something else!

Well, I should have known from the restaurant title because non-fish options were slim. Since it was kind of clear he was buying, I didn't want to order expensive shellfish. So when the server came, I felt I was able to procure a chicken dish I'd found at the very bottom of the menu.

I ordered the chicken.

Before I could finish the sentence however, the server named "Danette," said, "Oh...I don't recommend the chicken here! We're a fish restaurant."

I smiled feeling embarrassed a little, yet said, "Thank you for letting me know. Would it be okay if I still just have the chicken though?" She gave me a look that said, "Sure but you are freakin' NUTS." So then Jeff, who I'd just met, goes, "Who orders a non-fish dish in a *Fish* House?"

It hung there for a sec.

Nate rushed in to save his friend. "Uh yeh, the fish is really good here Robyn!" I couldn't believe it—I was being peer-pressured to eat fish. I was being ganged up on by two playground bullies to eat a scaly oceanic creature (which by the way, came here frozen, because this is Grand Rapids and there's no salt water within 1800 miles of here so I'm pretty sure, no matter how good the Mahi Mahi is and how non-fishy you insist it is, it's not even fresh, so I know it's not going to taste *that* good)! None of this I expressed out loud however. Out loud I said,

"Well...that's fine..." longing for it to cease to be an issue because I wasn't prepared to throw down over it—I wasn't allergic and it wasn't worth the embarrassment. So in a Betty-Draper-like manner, I finished the sentence while looking sweetly over at Nate, "What...what do you recommend?"

Bad. Bad choice of words. It turns out, I should have thrown down after all, because he ordered *oysters*. Now being peer-pressured to eat fish is one thing, but forced oyster consumption was a completely different matter! In a panicked internal craze, I ran a litany of options though my head: do I get up and walk out of here right now? (See how I learned to drive my own car to places after Car-lose?!) The other option was to politely refuse. It was after all only the appetizer, so since I had agreed to eat fish for the entrée, I'm sure they would be fair on the appetizer and give me a pass.

I chose not to walk out but to instead stay, and dangle my big toe back in the water.

The oysters were set down in the middle of the table. Nate, Jeff and Tonya all had googly eyes—they were clearly about to eat their favorite delicacy. I drank another swallow of my Kendall Jackson Chardonnay. They went around the table. I was stunned: these three grown adults slurped the oysters right out of the shell. Right then and there. No fork to plate. No knife to oyster. No cutting it into tiny pieces (which is what I was planning to do had I been pressured into it. Ya know how when you're a little kid, how you spread the food around your plate to get your parents to think you really ate it but instead you just gave it a thin distribution? That was my plan.) But NOOOOOH! Shell in hand: tongue out. Nasty slimy smelly RAW crustacean sliding down throats followed by guttural noises: "OH Yeh!" and "Un-huh!" and "That is sooooo good. Uggghhh."

Now, I have heard these sounds before in reference to food consumption and have even made these sounds before myself....over a bowl of ICE CREAM! Or Dove chocolate. But hearing these sounds in reference to raw seafood was all new. I guess I thought slurping oysters went with the shacks on the beach in Key West. There, I remembered tucking a paper towel in the rim of my t-shirt in order to protect against the dripping that came out of freshly boiled cajun shrimp because there was so much butter in it. On the beach, one had a bathing suit on under their shirt or cover-up, but these men were wearing ties...in Grand Rapids...in the winter...slurping oysters that were raw, unbuttered, unsalted and therefore unflavored.

So it became my turn to slurp an oyster because by now I had figured there was no way around it outside of storming out. I tried once more to pass on the oyster but the three of them stare-glared me down. "You have to," they said. It felt like hazing. I'm getting it now—I thought I was invited here for a friend experience. But I was really invited for a fish experience! That's where I'd made my mistake.

I slurped it down and tried to be a good sport because these seemed like the type of people that would not only pressure you into something nasty but would call you a priss for not being happy about it. So I played along: "Hmmmm. That was delicious!" I lied. Then of course they asked if I wanted more, but now I had the pride to confidently insist on "no, but thank you," since I'd appeased them once. They let it go. So, that just goes to show you that it WAS a hazing of some sort.

After that, I decided that I didn't quite feel the same about Nate. Oh...I was collecting data alright—Let's see:

Strike one: You live with your parents.

Strike two: You ordered my dinner like I was a housewife from the 1960's.

Strike three: You cared more about disappointing your buddy than you did me.

And four, (if that weren't enough): you peer-pressured me to consume an oyster!

As I drove home that night, I thought about the strange concept, that a woman of my age could somehow be forced into eating food she doesn't like. What was wrong with me? But in the end, I had chosen to suck it up (no pun intended) and not let the potential fallout turn into invested shrapnel. So in looking back, I did make a choice that represented growth. But the idea that this was the best he could do to impress me? Ay. Yi. Yi. And to think I allowed an evening away from my homework for this and I had to get up early to make it up? Damn.

So, I didn't contact Nate for a bit. He of course kept calling and leaving me messages, and I of course now know I should have been more direct like, "Dude—this isn't gonna work out." But I didn't want the conflict. So I answered the phone only about every seventh time he called, nor did I initiate a call to him.

But: I felt a little tormented by Penny's advice and the yuck of this dating crap. I knew there was truth in what she said, but geewillickers—do I really have to keep doing this?! And yet, because I couldn't decide which I should want more, loneliness or companionship (the cost of loneliness being high to me and the cost of of dating these crazies also high), I err'd [Shakespearian spelling intended] on the side of companionship. And you guessed it, I gave him another chance.

In order to remain unlonely and continue to see Nate, I decided there would be no more group dates. I might see him for wine after the National Anthem or at a coffee shop on the weekends, but I was finished eating raw sea animals. "He doesn't do well in groups," I'd concluded. If we're talking forever-after, I'd reasoned this wasn't a favorable attribute. But for the next month, I could work with it.

And that's how it went. He called me—we met for coffee or wine (please notice: beverages only). Sometimes I answered the phone. Sometimes I didn't. It was casual because I was making it casual. I figured he'd get sick of that and eventually stop calling, but he surprisingly didn't. I figured that having coffee on Saturday afternoon was better than being entirely alone with my English textbooks. But I think he knew he had crossed a line with disguising the "Fish" experience as a "Friend" experience, so he didn't push me.

When the holiday season rolled around, he told me he was going away and he expressed that he was very sorry about "being gone on Christmas." I was not sorry, but I kept this to myself—you know, it was good diplomacy. Anyway, he explained that they were going to Decorah, Iowa, and it's where the "Swedish" celebrated Christmas and that he was going to visit along with his parents, the Petersons from his mother's side, even though his last name was Peterson from his Dad's side. "Your mother and father had the same last name when they met?"

"Yeh...but it's not what you think! They're are not blood relatives! There's are just a lot of Petersons in Iowa. You know....it's like 'Smith' or 'Jones.'" I tried to respond jokingly:

"It's a good thing...'cause that would have been a deal breaker!" ha. ha. ha. He nervously laughed. The poor guy. Do you know how many times he'd probably had to explain that? It did sound a bit rehearsed as if he'd told it a gazillion times. He finished talking about Christmas and explained more about the trip and about how he would be gone for New Year's too, and that he would be getting back the day after and that they would go to Swedish shops and huddle around roaring fires with spiked hot cocoa and that he'd sleep on the floor at Aunt Lillian's and it was a blast, because they all crashed on the floor together. Wow. Yes, sounds like a blast—this would explain the "spiked" nature of the hot cocoa. I covered my mouth as not to expose a yawn on my side of the phone.

"Have fun," and "Merry Christmas!" I wished him.

"Thanks, you too. I'll call you from there! I will miss you so much..."

"Have a great time!" and I awkwardly hung up the phone because the longer I was on, the better the chances were for me having to respond with "I'll miss you too." I knew I wouldn't miss him.

So, while Nate was gone shopping in quaint Swedish shops, drinking spiked hot cocoa and sleeping on his Aunt's floor, I had a chance to zoom out. It was a chance for an epiphany of great magnitude to take place and so here it is:

Please pause for a sharp intake of breath (or conjure up imaginary drum roll in your head......... Ba-dump-tishhh....)

I didn't like him.

Profound. In fact, no more profound words were ever spoken from my subconscious to my conscious brain. It was liberating to realize that I'd actually rather be lonely than to have his company. In fact, I wasn't even lonely: I was just by myself...and...I kind of...liked it. Oh, I knew I wanted to get married someday, but to a Good Knight! Nate wasn't a bad guy. He just wasn't my knight (and for the record, I'm still not over the oyster slurping. It still feels like it's crawling down my throat whenever I think about it. So for that, my experience with Nate did leave a lasting impression.)

But because I prided myself as having class and wanted to handle it as elegantly as I could, I thought I might continue to hang out with him as a friend, but that I didn't have "girlfriend" feelings for him. It was weird to be the one saying, "We can still be friends." No one wants to hear those words because you know you're not going to remain friends. It's a way to let people down gently. There was a guy named, "Stephano," I really liked who said we could still be friends. I had told Burk we could still be friends. I did not tell Car-lose we could still be friends, however, and at least the Lug for all his faults, wasn't acting like there was a snowball's chance in my toaster oven to remain friends. Yet with Nate, I kind of meant it. I would have still liked to have coffee or wine, but as friends—not more.

Since I was broke that Christmas (full time college—3 part times jobs), I made Christmas cookies to put in decorative tins for my friends. It's so cliché—baking Christmas cookies. I hated clichés, but it's what broke people give at Christmas (unless of course you receive cookies in addition to other gifts—then it's fair to assume the giver isn't broke. But in my case, it was the only gift so it was a fair assumption.) I was planning to make more elaborate gifts than this for my family and also planned a trip to TJ Maxx to find something special for Jeannine and I knew TJ Maax would assist in helping me find one beautiful treasure with a friendly price tag. But all of the rest of my friends got cookies. [By the way, these days most of my friends and I give each other the beautiful gift of not having to get each other anything. I love that at Christmas now.]

Nate called a few times from Iowa. Sometimes I answered. Sometimes I didn't. He said he had found me a gift, and he said it in this adoring way that made me a little scared, like... "I'm-in-love-with-you-and-I-can't-wait-to-present-my-gift-to-your-adoring-reciprocal-love..." scared. I had been putting the signals out for over a month (ever since the oyster incident) that I wasn't prepared to go hot and heavy, that I was going the other direction. I was taking pains to communicate those to him, such as no kiss good night—no hanging out at my place—no commitment for next weekend's plan. It turns out that I should have been more direct. No, not more direct—just plain old direct in the first place.

I hooked up with him to give him his tin of cookies after the hockey game during the first week of January. The timing was the first problem—ya know how the festive spirit of the holidays usually leaves you right around oh...the first day of January? Sometimes it's even a push to do a gift exchange between Christmas and New Year's and expect that festive energy to still be around. In case you were wondering, there was NO hustle and bustle in the atmosphere around us with which to take the awkwardness out of exchanging gifts. So, that was the first problem.

The second problem: remember, People, I made him cookies. Just cookies. I was expecting him (before he called with the luuhhhhhve in his voice) to exchange a similar gift...or even nothing would have been fine. Because I wasn't expecting a lavish gift, I was trying to keep the exchange casual, which is why we met at the wine bar for one.

He was already sitting there when I blew in along with my decorative tin of week-old Christmas cookies. Nate was occupying a high-backed booth that was romantically tucked away: The situation said, "Come...linger with me for awhile." I had been hoping for more of a belly-up-to-the bar dynamic because it suggested a quicker date. I took an inward breath to brace myself for the "lingering." He jumped up and gave me this enormous hug. I tried not to hug him back too much. Once I sat down, I realized that he was seated next to this enormous gift bag. "I am so excited to give you this present," he declared, with an expectant light in his eyes, as if he were a child. I was immediately unnerved. What was I supposed to say in return except, "Here's your cookies. Sorry they're stale. Happy...umm... New Year?"

So, he hands me a gift bag that was enormous: it was actually so large that it had to be slid across the table. The bigger and bigger statement this gift made, the smaller and tackier my tin of cookies became. Could I magically snap my fingers and make a nice dress shirt appear in a wrapped box? Uggghhhh.

Inside were two Swedish hand-blown crystal wine glasses by a company called, "Orrefors Crystal." They were gorgeous. They were pure lead crystal and the stems were bright royal blue. And that's right: he had left a price tag on the bottom of one of the wine glass boxes (they were individually wrapped) and it said $70.00. Seventy dollars for one wine glass? And you got me TWO of them *and* a bottle of 25-dollar bottle of Chardonnay (I knew the brand). That's One HUNDRED and SIXTY-FIVE dollars, not including tax.

Nate lived with his parents...did THEY pay for these? Trust me: he didn't get these at a discount store. The way they were wrapped reeked expensive little quaint shop in Swedish Iowa. What's my problem you ask? Why wouldn't most girls want to be given a lovely gift like this? Here's why: because I knew it wasn't free. It came with strings attached.

I didn't want to be attached to him because the glasses were beautiful. I'd fallen for that with the Lug so many times! Now: I know Nate wasn't trying to be intentionally manipulative like the Lug had been with his luxurious gifts. I'm sure Nate meant it to be generous and that's it. Regardless of Nate's intentions though, I sat there... astounded, in an awkward empty wine bar on a Tuesday night in January at 7:45 pm and I couldn't match him in either arena: the gifts or the expectations.

So, I did what any disappointed girl in my position would have done: I faked appreciation. "Thank you" and "...that was so thoughtful" came dripping out of me. "I'm sure I will use these a lot and well....you know that wine will be gone before you know it, eh?!" It wasn't until later that I realized it was worse than even that: he wasn't giving me wine glasses for me to use on my own time in my own home. As if painfully watching a moment that might have been otherwise prevented and inwardly shouting a slow-motion "NOOOOOH," it dawned on me that it was gift to *us*. It was a bottle of wine and *two* glasses to share to-geth-er. Duh.

I stammered and handed him the cookie tin, "Merry Christmas and Happy New Year." It was hor. ri. ble. He accepted it with grace but I'm pretty sure he was disappointed. Big Sigh.

So, home I went with my designer crystal wine glasses and he went home with his cookies. It was such a crazy moment, that I let him think it wasn't our last date. I didn't kiss him or let him kiss me. All I wanted was to get outta there.

I wrote him a thank you note. It was a very sensitive gift after all. I loved chardonnay. We drank wine together and it was fun sharing that interest with him. So I did have legitimate stuff to include in the note.

I was terrifically embarrassed however, a few days later, to have also received a handwritten note from him thanking me for the cookies. (That was back when people didn't combine professional and personal email messages. Nate only had email at work. Yet still, exceptions could be made and it would have made me feel so much better had he just shot off an email thank-you.) The gift he'd received from me required nothing more. And frankly, Jeannine and I had called "bullshit" on thank-you notes a long time ago. We agreed that if the person receives your gift while you are present and you say thank you to their face, it should be enough. You have verbally acknowledged your appreciation. We agreed handwritten notes were gratuitous. We'd included a clause for the health and well being of weddings and funerals, of course, but friends and family who are in the same room? Peeshaw!

I had made an exception with Nate and the wine glasses though, because I did think it was a kind gesture even though I had preferred he hadn't at all. But I poured over the note to make certain I hadn't included any leading language. How does one sound grateful without leading language unless you sound like you're writing to your grandmother? It was a tough balance. But I managed it eventually.

So, that My Friends, is the story of Nate and the crystal glasses, oyster slurping in Fish Houses, Decorah, Iowa, an inappropriate gift-exchange and stale cookies. All that from one guy I *sort of* dated for two months. With great tact however and later on in my life when I could afford it, I added to the collection of the Orrefors glasses, because I liked them so much! But before you judge me, allow me to remind you that Penny told me as per her advice, that trying out guys (going out with anyone and everyone who asked) could yield a blessing from time to time, even if I didn't end up liking him. I think she meant a free dinner, but hey: I had barely gotten that with Car-lose, so as tacky as keeping the glasses were and tackier still adding to the collection later on, I figured that fate owed me.

Six:
Skipper and Delbert

Ahhhh, Skip. The name "Skip" conjures up a fun, sexy dude, 'doncha think? I don't know—I've just always liked the name. But I met Skip in the most unsexy of circumstances which is why I'm not so sure it's a "sexy name" anymore. But ya know what English teachers say? Connotation is everything! The ideas, memories, or experiences you bring to a word or a name, defines the meaning of that particular word or name, as much as the denotation (which is just a fancy term that means it's the Webster's definition).

I heard that..., I heard that sharp intake of breath you just took! You are fascinated and thrilled by this news and you're also welcome for the mini English lesson. But the English lesson isn't my point. My point is that I am apologizing in advance if I am about to ruin the name, "Skip" for you. Maybe I don't have that much power since you could be feeling, "Go for it Robyn: I dare you to try. My Skip is an awesome Skip—my Skip is a Dude!" or "My connotations for Skip are fun and energetic, prolific and tutorial!" ...which, I have no idea what any of that means.

Here is my point and why "Skip" could now be a downer name for you: I met Skip...wait for it...in...[please envision the scary epic motion picture music]...dum Dum DUMMMMMMMMM: AMWAY.

Yes, I said Amway.

No, I'm not claiming it was cool.

No, I'm not suggesting you should sell Amway.

And no, I'm not saying Amway and or the selling of Amway hasn't changed for the better and if you're currently doing it and liking it, that you should stop selling Amway.

These disclaimers have now concluded. Thank you.

But Yes, I had a dream. Yes, I showed the plan. Yes, I read "books" and listened to "tapes" and went to product pick-up. Yes, I had a downline and an upline. Yes, I dated Skip and he was "crossline," oooh oooh ooooh! This was a no-no because it was considered "not duplicatable;" unless you were already married, dating in Amway was frowned upon because it might distract you from "building the dream." But I dated Skip anyway. Now if any of these terms/phrases I just mentioned mean nothing to you, no matter. You will enjoy this chapter and should absolutely not skip Skip. But if you do know what phrases like, "show the plan," "upline/downline" "dream" and "duplicatable" mean, you will especially enjoy this chapter because now I am your simpatico sister. To the other contingency of readers foreign to the heretofore vocab words, stay tuned and be thankful you were spared or that you spared yourself as the case may be. Be thankful you don't know what Quicksilver is.

So, I met Skip at an Amway function. He was really handsome and was always wearing a suit (because that's the Amway way—for men to wear suits to every event and for women to wear skirts and dresses... at least it was then). He kept looking at me and I kept glancing over at him and then I began asking myself if that guy might be staring at me? Or does he just think I'm staring at him? Weird. But, like I said, he was handsome—a little clean-cut perhaps, but definitely good-lookin' with a nice smile. There were hundreds of people in this banquet-hall-style meeting room and quite honestly, he could have been looking at anybody.

A little while later and confirming my suspicions, a guy in my upline came over and said, "Hey that Skip guy wants to know if he can have your phone number. He's interested."

"I thought that was a 'no no,' consorting with crossline folks!" He shrugged, "Well, yeh it is but you're a pro and as long as you don't discuss your business with him, it will be fine. I mean, it's not like you're going to get married or anything!"

To myself: Oh yeh?? Everyone's a prospect these days, Dude.

So I handed my upline friend my business card which had my Amvox number on it. Amvox was a voicemail exchange messaging system where no one actually had to talk to a live person. A nice lady like Siri answered and told you how many messages you had and from whom, so it was a completely safe way for me to interact I figured.

So Skip amvoxed me (yes, people, before the verbs emailed, Face-booked, and texted, there was the verb, "amvoxed.") He sounded really nice and so I amvoxed him back. We amvoxed each other for a couple of days.

It turns out he lived on the other side of the state and in addition to "building the dream," Skip was in school for his MBA and also worked at a gym where he built his own body and trained others to build their bodies. Come to think of it, he was a little obsessed with body building. But he looked nice, so who was I to complain if he had big guns? Since we didn't live near each other, the reality was I didn't see him much at first, except at regional/national functions because between both of our day-job schedules, in combination with our intense focus on "building the dream," we didn't have time for much dating outside of the "business." We talked on the phone a lot and spoke goo goo crap to each other and both of us thought we were really onto something (how could I find a good-looking, responsible smart guy at 30 who was still single? How could he find the same in a woman who hadn't been divorced twice who didn't already have three little kids? We had standards, you know?)

But anyway because of the long distance build-up and the lack of being able to see each other outside of the biz, we finally took things to another level at The Free Enterprise conference in Charlotte, North Carolina. Free Enterprise was an annual Amway function for the serious leaders who had the commitment to drive in an economical car the size of a can for 20 hours, crawl oneself out of a pretzel-like state, endure all of the expense for the emotional, financial and physical toll, only to arrive and share a hotel room with ten other people (in order to share the expenses you know, since we were all broke which is why we were "building the dream" in the first place), only then to somehow find a way to shower, change, look presentable as a business person ought and then go to rallies in a stadium that had motivational speakers...many many many motivational speakers and listen to the same chick at every one of these rally-type events come out on to the stage and sing "all fired up fired up fired up."

Also, there was this agonizing [aka STUPID] unspoken contest about who could stay up the latest. It was expected that if you were serious about your goal to be independently wealthy, you had to learn how to be gritty and strong. Although this was never officially announced or written down in materials, it was absolutely understood by everyone in attendance who wasn't brand new. By staying up until 3:00 am to wait for a guy named "Dexter" to come speak motivationally about how he was the biggest baddest Amway-plan-shower on the face of the Amway earth and how listening to *him* would make you successful by showing *yourself* how much you cared. Yes it would! Staying up until 3:30 am, listening to Dexter was supposedly bootcampish-like training "for when times get tougher," your upline would tell you. "If you can do this now, [sitting here until your panty hose become one with your flesh], you can do anything, People!!"

I disagree. Amway functions, as grueling and as boring as they were, did not, for example, make childbirth an easier experience for my Amway girlfriends, you know, because *they had been prepared* for tough times by Amway and well...Dexter. Regardless, everyone in attendance tried at first to stay up, but then began dropping like flies around midnight until one by one, the distributors would make the walk of shame to the elevators. By 3 in the morning, there were a few proud distributors left, sitting there gallantly like twenty-five pound Tom Turkeys. The problem for big proud Tom Turkeys is that five minutes after they realize it's time to strut their stuff, they find themselves beheaded, horizontal, trussed at the ankle and steaming hot on an holiday platter for someone else's consumptive enjoyment.

But all I fundamentally knew at the end of sitting through hours of trying to believe I would eventually someday *make* some money, was that I better at some point, also someday, get these pantyhose peeled off of the backs of my thighs so I could restore feeling to them, dammit. Don't get me wrong, some people actually made money doing Amway. I just never did, and I was beginning to get to the point with it [two years in] where I believed I never would, and Y'all? I had given it the old college try for sure.

So it's not shocking then, that Skip and I found attraction for each other, especially at Free Enterprise in North Carolina. We'd both crawled out of separate tin-can cars, were sharing rooms with ten others, yet showed up at the rally trying to look professional and motivate our downlines. But later on when our downlines disappeared to go to bed (essentially middle-fingering Dexter, because really the few that did not, should have—it was late and BORING and he had this long frizzy beard—which by the way, violates the Amway facial hair code of ethics that men should not wear facial hair. I concur with Amway on this one: I don't care for facial hair either, Duck Dynasty popularity these days or no Duck Dynasty. I don't like it, never have and never will—but somehow crazy Dexter got a pass even though he was the died-in-the-wool-Amway-sellin' king! He had a weird gleam in his eye—it scared people. It scared me. It scared Skip...), so we snuck away for a tasty fourteen-dollar burger in the lobby. (Fourteen dollars each mind you—sold to starving broke people who were trying to build their Amway business on a dream. That's not all—it was a CRAPPY hot-lunch, quality burger. Ya know how hot-lunch burgers taste like there might kind of maybe be some beef in there somewhere, but it's really some bread crumb mixture to stretch the meat and make it *seem like* it's a burger when really it's just a McHockey-Puck? That's what it was like.)

It was our first date: twenty-eight bucks on hockey-puck patties in a corridor of the Charlotte Coliseum in Charlotte, NC. Skip paid. He wouldn't think of it, of making me pay for my own—even though this was a business meeting. After choking down our patties with five-dollar bottled water, he looked at me, cocked his head to the right and said, "Wanna get outta here?"

I raced him to the elevator! Now, here's the thing: you know I'm not *that* kind of girl, you know that I wouldn't go sleep with a guy after a few amvoxes and a couple of choked down gravel patties. But I am the kind of girl who gets exceedingly bored at Amway functions, whose not into Dexter, and who does know a cute guy when she sees one. I figured ANYTHING I could do with Skip, even if it were only reading comic books and/or finding a couple of beers in this godforsaken place would be better. So we ran for the hills or er...our separate, very private Holiday-Inn-Express hotel rooms, tripped over our separate, very *un*-private suitcases that were lined up in rows on the floor, and while stumbling to find our own, simultaneously changed into sweats and tee shirts with a promise to meet in the banquet room down the hall which was dark and evacuated.

I arrived one minute before Skip who, to my pleasure and amazement, was carrying a 6-pack of Miller Light. Ahhhhhhhh—Nectar. Of. The Gods!! "Where pray tell, did you procure that??"

(Amway was a business meeting remember? It was ALWAYS and forever dry—no open bar ever. No cash bar ever. No. Bar. Period. Sure there were lounges in some hotel lobbies, but those were for the "uncommitted members" who were considered seedy types. 'Not for respectful business people like Skip and myself—or so we had let everyone think!)

My question to him WAS a fair question of amazement mixed with being impressed—you can't know how many times Cole, Jeannine and I had wandered by concession stands when the arenas we were inhabiting, otherwise used for hockey games or various other sporting events, were closed. There it was: a Budweiser tap—stone cold EMPTY. Now *there's* something I would have paid fourteen dollars for at an Amway function!! And please believe me when I say this—I don't even really like beer! This is how desperate we felt at these events (...we were victims to our financial brokenness, see, so we believed at the time it was just part of the bad that comes with, what we were told was, inevitable good.) So, I desired beer when I didn't even especially like beer. Beer meant fun—it mean party—it meant that we weren't all taking ourselves too seriously. Dudes: there was never beer. I know you're feelin' my pain here, which is both literal and figurative. The beer represents anything other than an Amway "business" function!

Back to Skip and his 6-pack: Skip smiled holding his 6-pack with pride: "I snuck it in and my upline didn't see it and neither did my downline. I packed sweatshirts and shoes around it in my suitcase. Pretty sweet, huh?!" Right then and there I thought I would absolutely marry Skip because Skip was like a magic airline employee who offered you a hotel after a 20-hour storm delay when you've been stuck in airports. If the bed is lumpy and the motel is in a bad neighborhood, you don't care—it's just heaven to lie down. This felt the same: handsome Skip, no Dexter, no sticking panty hose, a vacated banquet room and beer. Does it get any better?

It actually did get a little better because although we were occupying an otherwise occupied banquet room, we didn't think it would last. Surely some security person would come along and kick us out. Surely the party who had rented it would come along and kick us out. Surely my upline distributors would come looking for me and we'd get caught (as if two grown-ups at 30-ish years of age needed to worry about that but we did...). Instead we had more cool stuff from "the gods." First the nectar and now unlimited privacy for hours.

We drank all of the beer.

We made out.

We talked.

We made out some more.

I looked at my watch telling me I should "get back" to my ten adult babysitters in the hotel room.

He talked me out of it.

We fell asleep (fully clothed I might add) on the floor underneath the banquet table, my head on his body built chest.

We woke up about 4:00 am and decided since the committed business associates would JUST be getting back from Dexter's speech, now would be a great time to go back and blend in (like we honestly could blend in wearing sweats and smelling of beer, and especially with my face all red from kissing his 5 o'clock shadow. But ya know— sometimes we have to just go with the logic that's available.)

He kissed me good night from behind the banquet room doors and we left separately and quietly like it was some CIA covert operation involving special forces. (Oh...there were special forces at work all right: they were called: beer, sweat pants and no Dexter!) Skip promised to Amvox me when he got home.

And so I thought about him the whole way home and to be honest, it took the edge off the trip. Of course I wasn't thinking about anything I had supposedly gone there for, i.e. making money (eventually), believing in myself, gaining strategies on how to build my business along with tips on how to prospect new enrollees. I just thought about Skip, the Miller Lite and the banquet room.

I did decide however, that if we were going to give this relationship a shot that we had to do it on some coattails other than Amway's. It was great to flirt and get to know him that way, having a solitary thing in common (even if we disliked the thing) in order to bond and take some of the awkwardness out of going on the traditional first date—you know, where one slurps an oyster, drives forty in a sixty-five, or hides their drunk date from sober church goers. I needed to see if our relationship had any meat on its bones.

So Skip made a trip over to see me a couple of weekends after that, and we went up north to Frankfort, Michigan to his family reunion. If you are going on a real first date, I not sure I would suggest making it a family reunion....if you can help it. But that's what we had so I was going with it.

On the ride up north, I asked Skip his parents' names, also asking what I should call them.

"Well, my Mom's name is Barbara and my Dad's name is Delbert."

Loud vinyl record scratching shock noise goes here.

My head whipped around and while simultaneously crumpling up my forehead, I asked back:

"Your Dad's name is Dil-BERT?"

"Uhhh...no. "Dilbert" is a comic strip in the Sunday newspaper. My Dad's name is '*Dellll*-bert.' " Thank goodness you clarified that Skip, as Delbert is of course *very* different than Dilbert?!

Then he shared another tidbit of special information, "Oh and my middle name is also Delbert. Skip Delbert!" He was smiling with pride.

Okay, Skip Delbert, I am going to take a deep breath. I imagined a yoga breathing pose and did a mental in-through-the-nose-out-through-the-mouth exercise so I could then try to muster the strength to also accept that I felt it was something to be proud of too. With a faint smile, I made myself look past it to his beefy broad shoulders and cut-up triceps. Yes—this will do nicely for a distraction.

Upon meeting Skip's dad, Delbert, although he was very nice, was exactly like he sounds: very...uhhhh...Del-ber-tee. His Mom was a doll too, but it started seeming like I was getting too much information abut Skip's family too soon in the relationship. His sister had been through a really hard time—a single mom with a five-year-old cutie pie, but it scared me because I felt dragged into too much intimacy before I was even sure of my feelings for him. Initial bonding with Skip was one thing, but going for a long walk in the deep, dark catacombs of his family's "stuff?" I didn't feel certain enough of him yet and didn't want to be perceived by Skip, or his family, as having already glued myself to him.

Here's what I mean: I hadn't told Skip word one about my older brother Jef and the influence of that situation on my family which was enormous to me, and yet here I am sitting on the back stoop of his parent's house helping his sister process her divorce. Don't get me wrong, I'm a compassionate girl. And it is perhaps because I can't not help caring so much that I was learning to guard my heart, before I cared too much and couldn't get myself out. That's what happened to me with the Lug. It happened to me with another guy named Stephano. And it's not a situation at this juncture I would have chosen to put myself in. Can we just go out for some oyster-slurping perhaps and exchange some pleasantries before we bond over family pain? 'Just askin'. It made me too "in." Being too "in" would have been fine if Skip were the right guy, and the fact that I felt scared by being "in," is what first showed me he may not be.

It turns out, I could not wait to get out of there. The two days of barbeques, beach walks, family dinners, and therapy with Skip's sister finally passed, and I was grateful for the inside of his Chevy Impala and an end to my entrapment. We zoomed down US 31 and around me were familiar sights, like exits with gas stations that had suddenly become like long lost friends. Can you imagine?? Oh Shell at exit #54, I've missed you so! Darling Mobile at exit #62, there you are—I thought I'd lost you! BP—Oh sweet, sweet Beeee Peeee at exit #70: I never thought I'd see you again! Whew! There's nothing like old friends.

My personification of the gas stations also told me Skip wasn't a guy I was crazy about. He'd tried at one point to make a move on me behind the maple tree in his parent's backyard just behind the tire swing. I politely wriggled out of it and explained I was uncomfortable because Delbert could be looking on from the slider on the back of the house. Come 'on People—we all know if I'd been hot for Skip, I wouldn't have cared about Delbert and I wouldn't have felt uncomfortable. I mean, I trust I would have used some decorum, but I wouldn't have cared about kissing him in front of old Delb. Skip broke my rampant thoughts as we drove by exit #73 and an Admiral Petroleum I'd just given a silent shout-out to. He said, "Hey...uh...I was thinking...I don't have to be in Livonia until 8:00 am. I could make it to work if I left by 5 am without any trouble. How 'bout if I stay at your place tonight!"

" Oh...er...yeh...thank you...for....thinking of me [...thinking of me? What was I in need of, get well wishes? Was it my birthday? Why did I just say, "thank you for thinking of me?"]. I...can't tonight....I have to 'show the plan...' " It was a bold-faced dirty lie. It was an effective one however, because when an Amway distributor says to fellow Amway distributors that they can't make a social invitation because they have to "show the plan" or "I have to spin the circles," other Amway distributors don't only just understand, they roll out the red carpet. Disclaimer: do not use this lie to get out of any other social event. If you do, your friends, family and significant others will not only fail to understand, but they will berate you, call you "brainwashed," and consider having you committed. Conversely, the nutsos of your Amway peers will not only be impressed, they will encourage you to drop social engagements. In fact, they'll even support you in saying no to family weddings and bar-mitzvahs in favor of showing the plan and other Amway activities. Un-Amwayed people will never get it, so don't use this lie unless you know what you are doing.

I knew what I was doing. If the new Robyn were to look back, she would just say, "no thanks, not tonight, Skip." The new me would even let it hang there...in silence...until the other person feels awkward enough to drop it or rushes to change the subject. But I was desperate then to have people, in this case Skip, not push things because I was afraid of being talked out of my "no." This is what happened with the Lug. I tried to break up with him for five of the seven years we were together. For five long years I honestly tried to end it, but I was too easily manipulated. I meant "no" but he'd always wear me down. So lying was a newer tactic to avoid being talked out of my "no."

The truth was I did not have to show the plan and I did not want to show the plan: it was Sunday night and I wanted a bubble bath, some girlfriend chit-chat, a glass of wine ...by myself... and my own bed. ALONE! And just as I'd predicted, Ol' Skippy boy said, "Oh, I completely understand!" yet he was quick with the comeback, "What about next weekend??" So I was prolonging the inevitable of breaking things off, but the procrastination was fine with me since he lived three hours away.

He dropped me off, but not before we passed and I'd greeted and sent knowing eye signals to ten more gas stations, three Burger Kings, two McDonalds and one Taco Bell. Once home, he tried to linger but respected the fact that I had a "business meeting" to prepare for, so he settled for one kiss and pulled out of the driveway. "Thank the good Lord," I thought to myself, disguising a happy-wave. How did I get myself in these situations? Oh yeh...Penny's advice. I'd never meet a

Good Knight if I didn't date people. And the truth be told, I did think I was crazy about him as recently as Charlotte and the 6-pack. But now it was clear that the only thing we really had in common was Amway, and I had been slowly trying to wean myself off from it too. There had to be an easier way to earn "three thousand dollars a month." I hadn't gotten into it to get rich anyway—I just wanted to earn "three thousand dollars a month." But I had shown the plan thirty times per month—I was a Quicksilver for goodness sake (the formula for achieving the monthly three grand), yet I still wasn't making more than a couple hundred, which didn't even cover the costs of "required" books, tapes and functions. The motivational speakers on the tapes and at functions kept assuring me though, that this was because I was in the "building stages." Big sigh. "Maybe they're right. Maybe it's me? Then again, maybe it's not for me and this grass would be greener for someone else?"

I went in the house, went upstairs, started the bathtub water and came back down to pour myself a glass of Chard. I grabbed my handheld phone so I could call my friends from the tub. If Jeannine wasn't around, Jenny would be. So, I poured in the bubbles and got in, balancing my glass on the side of the porcelain tub (did I mention the house was a hundred years old?) and on the edge of my tile floor. Smart. But I did it anyway, making a mental note to purchase some plastic wine glasses...after I had made some money in Amway. I reached Jeannine on the first try:

"Hey Robbi, How was your weekend with Skipper? How was his family?"

"Well, his Dad's first name is Delbert, and I also found out Skip's middle name is Delbert."

"Delbert and Delbert?"

"Yep."

"Huh. Hmmmm. I really like Skipper and Cole does too, but I can't imagine you are liking him that much???" And ya see right there? That's what I LOVE about a girlfriend soul-sister. A girlfriend soul-sister knows you so well that you don't even have to tell her the whole story. She just gets it. Now, I would have loved Skip regardless of the Delbert/Delbert thing, if he'd been right for me, because all of us have crazy little factoids about ourselves and the ones we love, that we wish weren't associated with us OR them. I knew this truth, and yet just like that, because Skip wasn't the right guy for me, escaping the Delbert/Delbert situation was an element of enormous relief. Jeannine knew it. She didn't want Cole's middle name to be Delbert anymore than I wanted my future husband's middle name to be Delbert and his father's before him to be Delbert or come from a family with any Delberts whatsoever—wouldn't there be just a teensy-weensy bit of pressure on the naming of our son someday, if we were to have one?

And you know how people have finagled ways to take female names and make them into male names or take last names and make them into first names because they just can't live without that name in their family?? Like for example, my last name is "Brodie." If I had girls, then the last name Brodie may not stay with them, should they grow up and choose to take their husband's name. BUT, Brodie would be a GREAT little girl OR boy's first name for one of *their* kids!

I knew a guy once who swore that if he ever had kids, he would name his son Noah, because according to this guy, Noah of all the Biblical characters, had the most faith in the Bible. Can you imagine: "I swear Dudes, it's *gonna* rain!!" as he builds away on his ark, and his friends stand around besmirching him. That's what this guy explained was the reason that Noah had the most faith (and other than Jesus, I don't think I disagree). But anyway, he went on about this as much as I am doing here because he WANTED to name his son Noah. Well, he did in fact grow up and have a child. But he had a girl. So ya know what he did? He named *her* Noah anyway except that he dropped the "h," in order to spell it "Noa." I suspect he thought it was a little more feminine that way. At first I thought it was odd, but now that I'm an English teacher-writer-language guru, I think it's cool. Noa. But I was still scared at the prospect of baby Delbert.

My best childhood friend, Leesa and I used to lie awake in our sleeping bags on sleepovers discussing the horrors of someday ending up with a bad, bad very bad name (because back when we were twelve, we didn't realize we could grow up to keep our maiden names even if we got married, should we choose to like a guy with an unfortunate name. Our mothers changed theirs, so all we knew is we'd have to change ours.) "Can you imagine Robbi, my name being Leesa DinkleBauch?" Then I shrieked and said back,

"Holy cow, Lees—I could be Robyn Van Rompa!"

There really was a Van Rompa family and of all of the names I've changed for this book, in order to protect the guilty, Delbert and Van Rompa are not. They are original scary names. For goodness sake! What if your last name went from having a lovely sounding flow to it, to something close to, "Rumpelstiltskin?" Or worse yet, "Rip Van Winkle?" Let's try these together, shall we? Which of these names do you think sounds better for you, if you happen to be a real-life woman and not a fictitious character?

Robyn Van Rompa

or

Rip Van Winkle

Aha! Just as I guessed: NEITHER ONE! And I was supposed to live with a name like that? My twelve-year-old mind swore I could be a victim of this possibility. Most parents, if they are kind to their babies, spend months trying to come up with a first name that flows nicely with the second name. Yet, they put in all of that analysis, only for it to change in an instant the second a daughter gets married? It seemed ridiculously unfair to Leesa and I in our sleeping bags on the floor in her rec room.

And if I haven't yet convinced you that Delbert is a reason for a single girl to be scared, well then listen to this! My cousin just got remarried to a guy by the name of Rick Fogey. I kid you not. Good guy, Rick. Not so great a name. He's a good catch too as he is a cardiologist. He's a generous cardiologist too, this Rick; he travels to third world countries doing free heart procedures for patients in underprivileged communities who need help, all in his spare time. There is no question that my cousin found a Good Knight who is a great catch. But shockingly, she kept her first husband's name. She is not Fran Fogey but remains Fran Thomas, even though she married Rick Fogey, whom she is VERY happily married to. Thomas was her first married name. Now: if a girl remarries after her first husband passes, yet she keeps the first husband's name? Well, I'm just sayin' that I think even Fran *knows* that Fogey is an unfortunate name. In recent years his family has tried to explain that it's pronounced "Fo-ghét," trying to make it sound French. She calls him Dr. Rick "Foghét," but everyone suspects it's Fogey, as in "old fogey." My point is this: people who want a certain name, manage to GET that name or they go to even greater lengths just to avoid a bad name!

So, had I kept Skip on the radar, there was too big of a chance that I was destined to have a son and a grandson named Delbert. Worse yet, thinking again of the Noa example, I could actually have a daughter named "Delberta" or "Delbie" or "Delbertette" or some crap. Jeannine empathized with all of this, even though it remained unspoken. The fact that I'd only said, "His Dad's name is Delbert and Skip's middle name is Delbert" was enough. This means I didn't have to tell her the part where I felt I was getting too far into the family particulars too soon, or, that in the light of day when the Miller Light had worn off, I didn't really think he was that great of a kisser or that I'd unintentionally sleuthed out that his body was "built" and his hair was thinning on top because he took steroids. Ya know what they say about the other side effects of performance enhancing drugs? Well, I wasn't sticking around to find out if that part was true and frankly glad also that I didn't have to tell that part to Jeannine since she was a soul sister and "Delbert" had been enough. [Sidebar: if you don't know what I mean about the "other" side effects of performance enhancing drugs for body building, Google is your friend.]

For the record, I don't really like my own middle name. It's "Joy." When I was seriously pursuing a professional career in gospel music, my Dad and I talked about changing my name because although I liked my last name, Dutch surnames are long and have a lot of letters, many of them silent. It was confusing. My Dad said, "You could just drop our last name and be 'Robyn Joy.'"

I looked back at him perplexed, as a fifteen-year-old girl will often do when their parent makes a suggestion. While wrinkling my forehead and curling up the left side of my nose, I said, "'Robyn JOY?' Chirping for the Lord??"

"What's wrong with it?"

"Dad! My first name is 'ROBYN' for goodness sake....like the bird.... Helllllooooh??"

"Don't talk to me like that young lady and your name is spelled differently than a bird's and your mother and I did that intentionally."

"It *still* sounds like an effin' bird," I thought to myself, but given my skillful knowledge of what battles to pick with my esteemed father, I knew this wasn't one of them, so did not share this last thought with him. To this day though, if I try to reasonably consider "Robyn Joy" as a stage name, I fight the urge to gak.

So Jeannine got off the phone and said something to my brother like, "Robyn isn't crazy about Skipper," and Cole said something back to her like, "Damn!" because he really liked Skipper for me I guess. I think he was beginning to give up hope I'd ever find a Good Knight too. (I mean Skipper Delbert was a good knight I think—I mean, he was a fairly decent knight at the very least, just not one I could ultimately be happy with.) So, I spent the next week figuring out how to break up with Skip. Frankly, it would have been really easy to Amvox him and call it good. But my evaluative pendulum swung all the way in the other direction, figuring he deserved a face-to-face break up. But eventually I decided on a phone call, because it seemed it would be too cruel to him, to have him drive three hours across the state to get broken up with and then turn all the way back around. But if I went there, then he would maybe get excited about seeing me and then a break-up was just even more cruel: Hi Dude, here I am in person. It's over. See ya.

So after a couple of days I called him. It was disconcerting because I knew I'd probably see him at least one more time at an Amway function before I completely weened myself out of Amway. When we spoke, I could tell he was fighting a tear at the end of the conversation. Ick. I didn't like this. I wasn't good at this. I wasn't the Simon Cowell of break ups. I was the Blake Shelton: "Wow Man...I really lahk you...but for some reason there's just somethin' missin' for meh." I hated breaking up with people as much as I disliked being broken up with.

Seven: Hope Over the Toilet

"There's a sign over your toilet that says, 'Hope?!'" Jeannine was pointing and squealing at the hope sign...that was in fact... hanging over my toilet. Huhhh. Now that's interesting. I'd inadvertently hung a sign over my toilet that said "hope," and I hadn't even noticed it was funny until Jeannine pointed it out.

Yes, we are "hopeful" when we use the toilet aren't we? Big sigh.

I had just moved into my little house on Seventh Street. I was excited to decorate this adorable place, which was my first venture into home ownership. In my lonely singleness, putting a house together was actually the one activity I did by myself that brought me joy. I didn't enjoy eating alone, going places alone, seeing a movie alone, going to church alone, but decorating? It was my zen-joy, like....don't bug me—I'll ask you-for-your-input-if-I-want-it-but-I-probably-don't-want-it...joy. And this house especially was a peaceful zen-filled structure. It was a white colonial that was over a hundred years old. It had a roof problem, window problems and water in the basement every time it rained. It needed a new electrical work up and asbestos removal and of course, there was no air conditioning. But the charm of it outweighed all of the problems and if you've ever lived in a "happy house," you know what I mean. Some buildings feel oppressive to me when I walk into them—others are atypical. Unemotional. Yet, other buildings and houses offer a blanket of joy or peace...like there must have been, at some point, happy people that lived there or occupied the space.

When I came home, it was there waiting for me and when I walked in it every night, it gave my spirit a hug. My little white colonial on Seventh was my friend. Please resist the urge to stick your finger down your throat to gak at the sentiment, because I have some wine to go with that cheese! When I moved in, I was digging through my boxes and figuring out where to hang nicknacks and what shelves to display with picture frames. Because the house was old and had many families who lived there before me, there were already little hanging nails all over the house. So I walked in the bathroom upstairs; it was this quaint little room with black and white one-inch square tile, with an updated sink cupboard/counter combo and of course a toilet. Over the toilet there was a little tiny nail. I happened to be holding my "hope" sign. It's wooden, six-by-three inch, shabby-chic white, with a barbed-wire hanger. It was equipped with chubby small case letters spelling out in metallic silver paint: Hope. I thought, "Hey, that's the perfect spot for this little sign." I hung it there because of the size of the sign and the space on the wall: I did not make the connection to the humor or symbolism at the moment. I just hung it up and moved onto the next thing.

Now as a creative writer, I wish very much I could tell you that I also had a sign over the washing machine that read, "Pain." Or a sign over the stove that said, "Maybe someday if you're lucky." And a sign that said, "Good luck" on the refrigerator door (what can I say?! I'm Dutch. I had a difficult time throwing away food, even once it was bad. The fridge wasn't always a friendly place.) But alas, I cannot admit that I am THAT clever. I had one lettered-sign that said "hope," which I inadvertently hung over the toilet...and that's it.

The bathroom, you understand, is one's inner sanctum, especially the upstairs one where I showered. When people came over, they used the half-bath off the kitchen downstairs so no one ever really went up there, except my roommate du jour. Yet, one day when Jeannine called and said she wanted to come get the royal tour because, although she had been in and out on some quick occasions right after I moved there, she'd never seen what I'd done to decorate throughout, and she was excited to see it!

She stopped by on Friday afternoon of the next week and we were sauntering around. She was loving the little nooks and crannies of the old place, the built-ins and pictures I'd placed of she and I and of her dog and I and of her baby and I and of my Mom and I. (Funny when you're single, how many pictures of yourself you have up in your own house.) So anyway, we wandered upstairs and she peeked her head in the bathroom. She noticed the cupboard nobs I'd put on and said, "Oh my gosh, I LOVE those!"...And then her peripheral view caught the little sign over the toilet. "You have a sign over your toilet that says 'HOPE?' Bahahahahahahaha!?' "

"Holy Crap Jeannine [no pun intended], I DO have a sign that says 'hope' over my toilet!" We didn't know which was funnier: that the sign was there at all, or that I had not before now made a connection to the humor of wishing myself hopefulness when using the toilet?! Jimminy Christmas. How I missed that one I will never know.

One day I told one of the various bachelors about it, I think it was Burk, which launched a short conversation about how the human body doesn't digest the vegetable of corn particularly well. I fully admitted however, that I wasn't a nutritionist so maybe corn does digest well and just doesn't appear to. Burk said, "So the sign over your toilet says 'hope,' as in I 'hope' I don't see corn?"

I was never going to live this down, this Hope sign-toilet-entity deal.

But looking back over my life, I do think it is quite a fantastic metaphor for where I was then (in the bathroom...hoping not to see 'corn'...) Kidding—I digress. But anyway, I didn't just have hope for the bathroom, People: I still maintained hope for a Good Knight. I had hope for being unlonely. I had owned hope, had lost hope and had learned to re-hope again, for companionship, love and contentment.

What I found out about myself and the idea of contentment later on is that there is really no such thing as full-bore contentment; I always seemed to live with a longing for something more, no matter where I was in the development of any particular season of life. But before I had that epiphany, at the time I thought a Good Knight was going to solve everything, so I went onto hope for it like fumes left in the gas tank as you're inching and sputtering up to the pump after pushing your vehicle longer than you should have. I'd pushed my vehicle's fuel tank longer than I should have with the Lug, so now I was on serious fumes. (Seriously? Could I get a few metaphors in here?)

Back to Hope in the literal sense: it has been said that a person can live with out food for six weeks, yet without water for only three days. But a person without hope will die within minutes. Hopelessness is a state of complete and utter abandonment of comfort, whether it's comfort to one's soul, heart, mind, or body. Simply put, if you lose your job and then your house along with it, the lack of hope affects not only your emotional sadness, but your physical body as well, due to no warmth or shelter. Sometimes abandonment is self-inflicted and sometimes it comes as the product of being truly left by someone. In my case, it was a little bit of both.

Hope is important and it was important to me. Romantic poet Percy Shelley is one of my favorites with an interesting perspective on the topic of Hope. In his epic poem *Prometheus Unbound*, he said "...To love and bear; to hope until hope creates from its own wreck the thing it contemplates." Okay, speaking of bearing, please bear with me.

Here's the thing: Percy was a discerning guy who had been through some real crap in his own life. He was married twice, his first wife dying by her own hand. Both of his children also died. He was prolifically bullied throughout his life and eventually died in a shipwreck, all before the age of thirty. Surprisingly, in spite of his sensibilities and emotional flair, he was resilient in his findings about hopefulness, although it was indeed a knowledge he had to claw his way to get to. What Shelley meant, is that if we hope long enough, the emotional pain caused by the dashing of previous hopes will rebuild itself—it will come back around again. It's own "wreck," or mess if you will, will have a cell leftover on which to double and procreate new life for new hope.

So I was hanging onto Shelley's phrase—after seven years of hope and broken hope, two engagements and breaking it off once and then again, cat and mouse and mouse and cat, my hope had been spent. I was at a deficit for hope. I cried a lot. I longed a lot. I dreamt of security and had wishful thinking about someday decorating the Christmas tree with my little kids which should have been born already given the years of investment with the Lug. And once I finally managed to accept the truth that this relationship would be an epic destruction had I not pried myself away from it, I was thirty-two and feeling washed up. Dudettes, it was haaaarrrrrd.

But then?? I got my hopes back up after talking with Penny. Hope up up up and a date with Carlos. Hopes down—this sucks! Hopes up again—a date with Skipper and then another—hope's definitely increasing due to more dates with Skip. Ahhhh. Hope's down— aloneness back—hope fleeting.

And then there was a guy named Stephano. Hope obliterated. Dark days. I thought I was crazy about him, but in truth? I was crazy about the "hope" he represented when he came along. And that's why when it didn't work out, my hope was in a place of utter wrecked-ness. You'll see.

Eight:
COOL COLE
(He Ain't Heavy, He's My Brother)

By now, you are used to me nicknaming my old boyfriends to the point where perhaps this sounds like another one of *those* chapters. But in actuality, it's about...my BROTHER, Cole.

Cole is cool. Cole has always been cool. The term "bad ass" doesn't really begin to describe how tough and cool he is. His cool level is a cross between Arthur Fonzarelli and James Dean. James Dean because he's got a smoldering measured quality, and The Fonz because he has a goofy docile side. Cole's cool was easy for him.

Cole's rèsumè of cool includes building cigarette boats, racing cigarette boats, selling a cigarette boat to the United States Government for drug busts off the coast of Miami, a second degree black belt in Tai Kwan Do, several motorcycle and leather-jacketed incidences, not to mention he crawled out his window almost every night when he was 15 without getting caught. I'd hear him on the roof because my room was right next to his and think, "Ahhhhh—there Cole goes again...". I didn't really worry about him too much because I knew he could handle himself. He wasn't a bad kid really...he was a mischievous kid. What's the difference? Well, one *means* to do harm. The other one has naughty fun with a kick in his step.

Another element that made Cole cool was that when my Mom asked him about the shenanigans she suspected (which were admittedly only 5% of the ones that actually went on), he never lied to her.

"Cole—did you drink tonight?"

"Yeh Mom, I did." Funny how that worked for him. The truth is disarming. Most people expect a fib when asking that question to their adolescent, especially when said adolescent is not caught redhanded and can get away with lying. I do believe that if she'd known he was crawling out of his window as often as he was, the cool would have worn off because she WOULD have taken out a can of whoop-ass at some point. But as long as she only knew about a shred of his naughtiness, he could be honest about it to her face. Cole has been an honest guy ever since. He'll tell you the truth alright! And even in my jest, I was very respectful of his integrity. That was Cole.

So, how and why was Cole sooooooo cool all of the time? Well, I suspect he was a bit set up to be cool without ever having to try too hard. Here's why: our Dad married our Mom as a widower. He was married for 25 years to his first wife who passed from cancer at the young age of 45. My Dad (his name was Jack) had three daughters with his first wife. Then he met my Mom, nineteen years his junior, and had a second family. That's where Cole and I come in. And by the way, he was almost 50 when I was born (Rock it out Jack!)

But back to Cole's cool factor: so, my Dad was a manly man. He was cool too. He was a bad ass too. He was born in 1916, the fifth of six children. During the Depression he was just approaching adult life. He did things like: he drove a milk truck before school early in the morning when he was eleven to make extra money to help the family. By the time he got to be of college age, there was no money left for him to go to college, so he went into the family paper-supply business. With an excellent attitude, he decided to educate himself rather, and did so by reading thousands of books. He was also a World War II veteran whose musical skills kept him out of front line action; he was first chair on the Baritone horn in the Navy band. He had a kick in his step [Cole got it from *him*] and a positivity that was always unparalleled, so using his horn to promote morale in wartime suited him. This also satiated his Dutch practical side since his horn literally saved his skin. The day before his number came up to go into combat after two years in the Navy band, the war ended. My Dad had a light in his eye so unique, I'd only ever seen it in one other person when I was 32 and looking for a Good Knight: Cole.

Given that Jack had three girls, whom by the way he adored and loved to pieces, it's yet not a crime to begrudge a manly man a hearty son, so when my Mom found out she was expecting her first baby with Jack, everyone hoped it was boy.

"Jack will finally have a son! How exciting!" There was a lot of expectation put on Jack and his impending, maybe son. And it *was* a son. They named him Jef. The story goes that my Dad was indeed proud and beaming, and after nervously pacing in the waiting room next to the Coke machine and candy bars, got to hold his first son at the age of 48. Pretty exciting stuff. There was so much pride.

Yet, it didn't take long for my parents to figure out that Jef had some medical issues and before long, he was at every imaginable doctor's appointment. At four years of age, Jef was diagnosed at Mayo Clinic with "brain damage," decades before there was anything close to something called an "Autistic Spectrum." It was a complicated situation and it remains to this day a complicated situation. But at the time, my parents said it felt like all of the air had been squished out of a balloon.

Now, they dealt with it the best they could and had as good of an attitude as anyone could have. But by the time of Jef's diagnosis, I had already been born. I was two. The story then goes that one day when my parents were at a business conference, my Dad came in from throwing the football around with his buddies and got all [as my mother puts it], "frisky." (Really Mom, "frisky?" like...I'm yucked out that we even have to talk about this at all but if we are talking about it, do you really have to use the word..."frisky?") My Mom warned my Dad that if he proceeded with his friski-ness there was a good chance he'd have another baby. He didn't care. (Thank goodness she let the story end there without anymore details.)

Indeed, she was correct. So Jack had his sixth child. It was a boy and they named him Cole. So here's the gigabyte: a manly man *finally* had a "normal" son. It was the days before political correctness and that's what people said: Jef was the "handicapped" son and Cole was the "normal" son. Cole didn't ask to be the golden, normal son; it just happened to him. But you throw in my Dad's pride for "normal," a mop of blonde curly hair and piercing blue eyes and I'd say that Cole was just destined to be cool. His cool was the identity he was born into.

Cole's cool still goes on: one day recently when I was volunteering for parent/teacher conferences at the elementary school in our district, I was walking out and ran into one of Cole's kids' teachers. She looked at me dumbfounded:

"I just had a conference with your brother. It made me uncomfortable because: He. Is. So. Good-Looking. Wow...."

Right? Like....hellloooo....do you realize you just told me I'm chopped liver? Hellllooooh! It's okay, Loyal Readers; don't worry about my feelings because I'm totally used to it! I kind of respond like a pet owner would: "Your dog is adorable." Beaming, I return the compliment with a smile, "Thank you so much!!! Isn't he???" I'm not even kind of kidding—I don't take it personally. Cole is cool. Cole has always been cool. Cole is still cool.

What does Cole's cool factor have to do with my journey? Well, Cole is not just annoyingly cool, he was also a good brother. He supported me when he agreed with what I was doing and when he didn't, he made it known. Very, very known! He wasn't bossy, but when I was out to find a Good Knight, he was clear about who he felt was a good guy and who he didn't like for me.

Some may think, "Hey back off—this is MY life. I'll do what I want!" But Cole had earned a vote on it because he spent a lot of time protecting me from Jef's angry outbursts which were notably common, due to complications with Jef's impairments. Cole would drag me by the the arm into a closet:

"Shhhhhh. Leave the light off—he won't find us in here."

And there we'd sit, in the dark as little kids, hiding from a bully, who we were told couldn't "help it." Just the whites of our eyes shown, holding hands under the Monopoly box. Cole and I got really tight throughout our childhood because we were on the same team—we wanted to survive emotionally and physically. We did it together. I knew I could count on him, and I drew strength from knowing Cole was present. It was a comfort to be able to look at one person and see in their face, "I get you. I know EXACTLY how you feel."

Nine:
It's All Hollywood, Cool Breeze!

Yes, Carlos became known as "Carlose." For those of you who think this is unclassy, allow me to remind you that if we don't laugh sometimes, we cry, right? Nicknaming the Dudes who came and went helped me laugh. If I could keep them as characters in my own head, then I would personalize them less, and therefore not absorb the sorry state of things to the degree that it was. And it was very very sorry.

For example and on the subject of nicknames, Jeannine and Cole had a guy who lived across the street from them they called, "Crazy Neighbor." Crazy Neighbor used to sit in a lawn chair and water his plants: he would sit two feet away from the hemlock trees that lined his property and while holding a hose, he'd sit back in the chair, cross his legs in at the ankle and hold the hose as though it looked like an enormous arching phallic stream of urine coming from the center of his body. There are more examples of why they thought he had earned the nickname "Crazy Neighbor," but I think this is enough to sell the argument for the nickname, right?!

I used to know a girl named Becky whose father, (a class act who left her in a bar when she was eight so he could blatantly chase after some floozy while still married to her mother), remarried a blonde kitten thirty years his junior. Beck has called her "Do-Me-Debbie" ever since. This same friend had a new coworker hired in where she manages a retail store: Becky or er...Rebecca as she's known at work, being of Type-A mind and heavy discernment skills, couldn't help but notice what the gal wore to her interview: a plunging neckline and a push up bra. Nice, huh? She was hired by Becky's old man boss right on the spot. Ever since, Beck has called her, "Bimbalina."

And so it went with my former boyfriends and dates: the Lug, Carlose, Skipper [all hail to Gilligan's Island] and a gentleman I call "Rico Suave.'" Burk, admittedly remained "Burk" and was not assigned a nickname for whatever reason. There was also a guy named "Stinky," but that's irrelevant.

Sidebar: I'm sorry but I can't tell you why I nicknamed that one guy Stinky. Stop asking me.

But anyway, I was ready for a Rico Suave'. Rico Suave' did, in fact, have a real name: it was Stephano Ferrante. Stephano looked Italian. Stephano was drop dead gorgeously handsome like—pinch-yourself-I'm-dreaming handsome. He sounded sophisticated and looked classy; his name was Stephano Ferrante for goodness sake! I rolled the name "Robyn Ferrante" over in my mind a few times. I even said it out loud. I liked it! I could definitely tolerate being Robyn Ferrante!

I met Stephano on a flight from Cincinnati to Grand Rapids one wintry January night. I was actually traveling home from a vacay in Key West with....yes, you guessed it...the Lug. I know you're disappointed, but somewhere after I met Burk and after I went out with Carlose, I veered back to the Lug. He'd stopped over to my house one night while we were "broken up" when I wasn't expecting it, with the offer to fly me down to Key West for a "regatta" he was sailing in. I reluctantly thought, "Well, it's January in Michigan—he's offering a free trip to Florida. Why not?"

I'll tell you why not! I was re-entangled, albeit momentarily, to the same tiresome garbage. Do you suppose I had a little codependence problem with him? But whatever. On the way home, I had a flight that went through Orlando (I didn't stay down there for more than a couple of days while Lug stayed the week, justifying that "dabbling for a couple of days" was better than specializing in making it work for life.) My flight from Orlando to Cincinnati was delayed for (count them), EIGHT hours. So, out of boredom I went to get something to eat. I pulled my chair up to the table and at that moment, I caught the edge of my tray with the corner of my bag. It bumped into my diet coke and 28 ounces of wet, cold diet-coke fell straight into my lap, or I guess I should say....my crotch!

Cold and dripping wet, I went looking for alternate clothes to buy. Guess what's for sale to wear at the Orlando airport? That's right: MICKEY MOUSE adorned t-shirts, shorts, and sweatshirts. I was flying back into Michigan in January—I did not need Mickey Mouse garb to add to my wardrobe, but here I was desperate to wear anything else but these drenched leggings. Sadly, there were no clothing items to be be found that were not embellished with Disney-related caricatures. So I settled on a Mickey t-shirt and a pair of Donald Duck black gym-shorts. I was stylin' it out, my Sisters!

Finally, our flight boarded and I arrived with minutes to spare, in order to make the connection in Cincinnati. Take a moment and picture me: I had gone to Florida with my Michigan white skin for 2 ½ days. I had smudgey sun-burnish-trying-to-tan- skin in some places, but one of my cheekbones was more burned and splotchy than the other. The backs of my legs remained stark white, the fronts a little tannish-reddish hue. I had on the Disney adorned outfit I mentioned, but I'd also had one piece of my hair rattail-braided on Duval street in Key West. I was also wearing espadrille flip flops. It was a balmy 37 degrees in Cinci. I boarded the plane looking like a complete dork. But strangely enough, Stephano was on that plane. He talked to me from across the aisle, but I thought he was just being polite because he spoke to other people around us too. He told stories of the "Peabody Ducks" he had just seen earlier that day from the Peabody Hotel at which he stayed in Orlando and how everyday the Peabody Ducks would march through the hotel lobby. I thought, "Cute guy. Friendly." But I *never thought he* was noticing me! Besides, I was sitting there trying to figure out what the weekend with the Lug had meant. Did it mean there's still a chance for us? Did it mean, he'll really want to get married this time? Did it mean my eggs had a chance for fertilization if we got married by the next summer??

We landed in Grand Rapids and it was 24 degrees. We had an aircraft situation of having to deplane on the tarmac, which required walking down the aircraft's stairs, across a partial runway and then into the airport; I must admit this was a sporting event given the snow on the ground in my espadrilles. But I took it in stride in spite of my outfit; I was grateful for dry clothes, despite their minimal nature.

At the luggage terminal Stefano walked over and said, "Hey—uh—I think you're really cool. I'd like to take you out. May I have your phone number?" I. Could. Not. Believe. It.

"You want my phone number???"

"Yeh. I think it's cool you had on shorts but you ran out into the snow without complaining. Besides, you're really nice."

"I'm wearing Mickey Mouse."

"I'm sure you have a good reason," and he flashed a big grin—the Italian Stallion white toothy Matt LeBlanc kind. So I gave him my number.

He waited a bit, calling me three days later, which I eventually found out he did on purpose to make me think he wasn't interested. (I guess it's some kind of "man-code.") We arranged a date. But then? I started hemming and hawing. Ya see? The problem with every guy I met is that he wasn't the Lug, and the Lug, regardless of its dysfunctional craziness, was what I knew. So when the Lug returned from

Florida, he of course also called. I ignored the phone for the first two days it rang. Then he showed up on my doorstep with that wry smile and a bottle of champagne. I said, "Wait here." I went upstairs and called Stefano and told him I was betwixt and between (which was literal: Lug was on the doorstep and Stefano was in Grand Rapids at his apartment talking on the phone with me.) I explained my uncertainty over going out with someone new when I was still wrapped up in a old relationship; it was exactly like the decision I'd made a year and a half prior when I'd ended it with Burk at Christmastime. Then too, I scrambled back to the Lug, insisting there was still another shot for him and me. So, Stefano expressed disappointment and asked me to call him if anything changed.

And ya know what? After a couple of weeks with the Lug this time? They turned out to be the very last weeks I would ever spend with him. You thought it was never coming? Believe me, I never thought I could do it either. I called Stephano back and told him I was sure I was free to go out with him. He jumped at it and took me out the next weekend and after that our relationship was a whirlwind.

Stephano Ferrante became my boyfriend faster than an enthusiastic jackrabbit in springtime. He was everything: handsome, gentleman-like, fun, and he was six years younger than me. Six years. I was 33. He was almost 27. It was an interesting dynamic for me because the Lug was six years older, so I went from dating a 39-year-old to a 26-year old. Stephano seemed a tad bit (and I mean I only noticed a tad bit) immature, but he was new and youthful and I liked him, so I looked past it. I was tired of BMW's, alternative rock, and boutique wine. It was time to put the top down, zip around listening to Hootie and the Blowfish and stop off for a Corona with a lime.

Let's make sure we get it right about this Italian Dude from the start, People: Stephano was pronounced "Stef-fán-noh"—the accent was on the middle syllable, like a Shakespearian character. He was such a Stef-FAHN-oh too, every single bit as Italian as he sounded. I think in truth he had some German from his mom's side, but he wore the Italian only. Stephano was definitely eye candy. In fact, he was probably the most overtly good looking man I had ever met.

Adding to the fairytale-like nature of Stephano, I met his family and they were fantastic. They were just as Italian as I'd suspected, devoutly Catholic and completely lovely. In fact, they were sort of like the Italian families I'd seen in movies on Lifetime and Hallmark: loud, huggy, warm, great cooks and had a way of enveloping you so you belonged. I loved this about the Ferrantes! The Lug's family had been cold, distant, dysfunctional, unstable and downright weird. That's a lot for a girl to say, whose own parents were twenty years apart in age, whose older brother was severally learning disabled and emotionally impaired, and whose parents lived most of the time, like there was absolutely nothing wrong even though their impaired child had anger problems and, frankly, terrorized Cole and me. But whatever—the Lug's family won hands down for family weirdness. I am compassionate towards the Lug's mother though: she had five kids in seven years and she still lived in this tiny house she raised them all in. If I were shut up in a tiny house with five little kids after having been pregnant and nursing for seven straight years, I would have been crazy cakes too, ya know?? So although I was truly empathetic to the Lug's mom, his family situation scared me. Suffice it to say that when I met Stephano's family, I was tha-rilled.

And so it went, Stephano's and my courtship. We talked about marriage from the get-go. All of his friends accepted that we would probably get married. His family suspected it. They all knew my age and that of course I wouldn't be dating Stephano if he weren't serious about me. My family liked him too...that is...except for Cole.

Frankly, I was PISSED at Cole's initial response to Stephano. One Sunday after church (I had gone with Stephano to Mass), we met up with Cole and Jeannine after their service for lunch at Pietros in downtown Holland. We came in and after formally introducing Cole to

Stephano again (they'd met once briefly), we sat down in the booth. Cole, without skipping a beat, says, "So Stephano: how was that Catholic service you went to today? I mean...don't you get sick of that....stand up-sit down kneel–kneel–kneel...thing?"

Yes that's right, you read it correctly. My ever-so "cool" brother, of whom I was proud, loyal to and bragged about...just insulted my boyfriend's church affiliation and worship preference. To say I wanted to slap Cole and wet my pants at the same time isn't even close. I shot him a look that said "Who the hell are you right now?!" I was creating wrinkles in my forehead. Sharply, while trying to relocate my dropped jaw, I scolded, "COLE!!" What on earth–?"

Cole backed down. "I'm sorry Stephano," and he shrugged it off with a laughing smile. He stretched up his long mammoth arm and put it around Jeannine. She also shot him a look of disapproval. So Cole, beginning to sense the awkward nature of the interchange, said, "So.....how about them Tigers!" and fortunately the conversation drifted off towards baseball and other sports.

I called up Cole late that night after Stephano had dropped me off:

"Uhhhh Cole, what the hell was that?!"

"He's not the one for you, Rob." Cole absolutely didn't care that he had deeply offended Stephano or that he'd embarrassed me!

"What do you mean? How do YOU know?!"

"He's just isn't. You deserve better. Someone who is as smart as you–someone who can hang with you, someone who can go through the big stuff. Stephano's nice but, he's not mature enough or smart enough...or talented enough."

"Okay, now you sound like Mom regarding every other guy I've ever dated."

"Sorry–just telling the truth. Marriage is forever, Rob. You won't like him forever."

Solidifying Cole's opinion of Stephano is a little epithet I like to call "Cool vs. Cheese." It was a hot hot HOT September-farmland-central Illinois-kind of day. A couple of months after the restaurant horrification of Cole's insult, we had all gone down to a wedding reception for a relative on my side whose occupation was farming: thus, the location. Cole and Jeannine had decided to spend the night in Illinois that night, while Stephano and I had to return because I had an early class the next morning, so we drove in separate cars while caravanning through the farmland country roads.

Jeannine was five months pregnant and the air conditioner in their car went on the fritz in the middle of central Illinois and ninety degree heat. It had already been a long day getting there. We were still about an hour away when Cole called Stephano: "Hey Stephano, will you pull over? My AC is broken and Jeannine is dying in here. I need her to ride with Rob in the AC in your car, so will you come over and ride with me??"

Stephano hesitated.

Stephano didn't want to mess up his hair with the windows open.

Stephano was silently ascertaining the sweat/dust factor to his designer suit.

Stephano was unsure leaving me at the helm of his Chevrolet Monte Carlo.

Bottom line: it was NOT a chivalrous response. I mean seriously? Jeannine was PREGNANT?! What gentleman needs time to think about it??? Geeshh.

So Stephano, I imagine due to the peer pressure, finally responded with a reluctant, "sure." Cole pulled over and Stephano and his uncool walked along the shoulder of the dusty dirt highway and got into

Cole's Vovlo 850 Turbo. He kept looking down at his clothes to see if they were getting dirty or not. I had gone with him to assist Jeannine's transfer. As he got into Cole's car, Cole looked at him like, "You're such an asshole!" Stephano didn't know Cole was thinking that, but I knew that look!

Once we got on our way and assumed the course of our trip, Cole mentioned, "See Steph, not so bad now that we're moving along..."

"It's All Hollywood Cool Breeze." Cole turned, looked at him as though a blasphemous act had just been committed, and responded,

"Whut? What did you just say to me?!"

"Cool Breeze, Dude. You're 'Cool Breeze,' get it?!"

"Coooool. Bah-reeeeze?"

"Yeh Dude, it's a term of endearment!"

"And....the...'Hollllly-wuhhhd' part?"

"Oh, Hollywood just means 'it's fine'."

"Ok, so let me get this straight:... you've nicknamed me "Cool Breeze" but really all you were trying to say is 'You're fine with the car switch and not too hot?' "

"Yeh Dude!"

"Huh." Cole pressed his lips together, chewed a little bit on the bottom one while nodding in a methodical way and staring straight ahead at the country road.

And that was it: not another word was exchanged between them for the rest of the ride to the party. When Cole told me this story later on, I offered that Cole's shiver was caused by the degree of the comparison, you know, intense cool being in the same small space with such base utter cheesiness.

But ya know what? As mad I was at Cole about the insult at the Pietros lunch, something about what he'd said about "marriage being forever" began to ring true. He was right. Let's face it: Stephano was immature and not only a "tad bit," as I had reasoned out at first. I'd justified everything I hadn't liked, such as: staying out at a seedy bar 'til 2 in the morning and going out for bad pizza at 3 am with his fraternity brothers. (Yes, they were all long out of college, but still lived liked they weren't.) I had overlooked the stack of 25 Playboys his roommate left next to the bathroom toilet. I looked past the two softball games per week I was expected to attend so I could watch my "boyfriend" rub black ink marks under his eyes like a pro baseball player even though this was amateur, small-town softball.

And, I'd looked past it when he briefly mentioned he had thirty thousand dollars in credit card debt he had spent on....wait for it..... designer clothes, even though he lived in the upstairs bedroom of an old house with three other guys. [I'm not judging debt—I'm just saying, if you're gonna be thirty grand in debt to something at twenty-seven years of age, clothes are not perhaps the best security. How about an investment in your own...oh I don't know... PLACE? Maybe thirty grand would be better invested in a house?]

But, there was one event I had not looked past: I'd stood up for myself when I was expected to attend a Jimmy Buffett concert in Cleveland, Ohio, which was a mere nine-hour drive each way. I refused to be talked into sharing a hotel room with TWENTY other people. You know...because everyone is broke and all, it was explained to me that the lodging-portion of the venture would only cost five dollars per person! Given my tendency towards Dutch-minded frugality, one could not help but notice the fantastic savings this option provided. But, it was a non-option altogether, especially when it was also disclosed that sometimes the toilet gets backed up with twenty roommates. Yet, Stephano had been enthusiastic and steadfast with reassurance, saying, "It's okay Robyn, really—we do it 'cause it's FUN!"

Listen here Stephano, Rico Suave' or no Rico Suave': I am now 33 years old. I am not sleeping on the floor next to drunken, puking college recluses. You may. I won't. So his friends called me a Diva and a Bitch (even the girls). I didn't care. The concert was kind of fun I guess especially when Buffett played "Cheeseburger in Paradise," but ya know what? It's this exact experience that made me miss The Lug who preferred bistros over Buffett tailgating and his own hotel room over the community frat house. Yet, I reminded myself that there was absolutely no way I was going back to that Egyptian prison of bondage prior to the Exodus from the Lug. Stephano may not be the promised land, exactly, but he was better than the Lug—at least he didn't promise marriage and then retract. I was free to marry him alright and if he promised a hotel room with 20 people? Well, he was definitely going to deliver. If he promised softball games? They were definitely there. If he promised an Italian dinner at his Mom's? She cooked it alright!

Someone giving their word and then coming *through on their word* mattered to me, so I hung around. But after the the Buffett concert event, which was the first incident in six months of me saying "no" to anything, because I had stood up for myself regarding the hotel arrangements, Steph started to take some heat from his fraternity cronies—they started asking him questions like, "Are you sure you want to be tied down to someone who doesn't want to have the same kind of fun?" And really, why would *anyone* want their own hotel room and the privacy it provides?? I must be freakin' CRAZY Cakes!

Around that same time, I started back at college: I had decided that I wanted to change my career officially. The Ferrante family shared many beautiful qualities with me, but the most important was that they influenced me (without realizing it) to go back to school to get my teaching certification. It was an idea I had been tossing around for years. Stephano's sister Elena, had just finished her student teaching and his Dad was a middle school principal who'd spent twenty-five years in the classroom prior to his administration job. Their conversations and testimonies around family dinner tables convinced me that there could be joy in teaching. So, in the fall of

1999, I transferred my entire BA from the out-of-state college I graduated from ten years earlier, and began taking a full credit load towards a new discipline in English Lit. and Secondary Ed. I was full time with four Literature and Writing classes that first term. I was determined to get it done as quickly as I could, so I went about it in the non-traditional way: full time, year round. And I had three part time jobs which was the not-so-traditional part.

The point is, I didn't have time anymore to put up with eighteen-hour road trips to Cinci and arguments over hotel rooms with twenty-one roommates. Every spare moment I had was either in class, at work, or in a book. I could give Stephano and our relationship quality time, but not the quantity of activity that I had prior. So the first week of September in the fall of 1999, we went to the Michigan/Notre Dame game and of course I had to sit in the Notre Dame section. If it would be acceptable to put an emoji sad-face here like on Facebook or texting, I would include one. If you are from the state of Michigan or are a college football fan, you know what I mean. Enough said.

Suffice it to say, it was the last big event I went to with Stephano, but not because of the Notre Dame part; (sitting in the Notre Dame section was the cherry on top of what just added insult to injury). It was because of the Stephano part. Oh, I was still in love with him—I still wanted to be in relationship with him. But I wanted to steal an hour here and an hour there and make the most of it while I was in this new season of life. I couldn't lie around for six hours on Sunday afternoon anymore to random ESPN TV coverage. I thought he would support my endeavors because he'd claimed a gazillion times over that he was also in love and also wanted to get married, but when push came to shove, he didn't like the grown-up-responsible me very much. He had a difficult time grasping that I had my own life, dreams, and goals and I was willing to work my butt off to achieve those goals. He admittedly tried to hang in there with it for awhile.

Around the first week of October, he went three days without calling which was very strange. I tried to call him a few times. On the third day I reached him, and he was cold to me. Hmmmmm, I wondered. That's weird. I shrugged it off because I had a mountain of homework.

The next night I reached him on the phone before I ran into class. He said he'd call me when I got out. That night, over the phone, he broke up with me. He could not explain it. I asked him why why why? He said I was beautiful and he loved me and he just didn't know why but "the feeling was gone."

I got off the phone and to say I was shell-shocked was a misnomer. I was having my issues with the relationship as well, so my reaction to it surprised me. But I panicked! I threw up. I threw up for three days. I had panicky, around-the-clock, anxiety-filled rapid thoughts:

> I was thirty-three now. I was never getting married. I am never having babies. I am intended to be a spinster. It was a couple's world—a family's world. I knew that I was destined to continue to take care of my sick father who'd had a massive stroke ten years earlier, which had rendered my big, strong, competent Daddy into a sick old man who had no short term memory and little long term memory. (I'd helped my Mom out a lot over the course of those ten years, which I was happy and honored to do, but it was only because I'd *had* the time. Had I been married with children of my own, circumstances would have prevented devoting the time commitment she needed/wanted. As much as I loved my Dad and was proud to assist, it represented my singleness in a way I didn't like.) Stephano has walked out; this means my Dad would live another ten sick years and all I'll have to show for my life was his care. There are worse things, certainly, yes, but this isn't my dream! What will I be now? What will I be *worth* now?

All of these hardened thoughts came crashing at me, each taking a gouge and leaving a mark—although I tried to shield them as though they were incoming shrapnel, I couldn't protect myself from all of the negativity. If you think of these thoughts as ammo, I was so bleakly struck, I felt like I'd lost a war.

I called Stephano the next morning, and told him to please come get his stuff, and that I wanted it out of my house as soon as possible. I didn't want the memories around controlling me from a box on the floor in a corner. I told him I had class that night and after that I had to sing the National Anthem at the IHL hockey game; I asked that he please come while I was gone and explained I wouldn't be home until 9. That afternoon before class, I took three Excedrin. Okay, don't ever do that. I wasn't used to that much caffeine and I had the emotionally-exhausted-wired crazies. I'm not sure I've ever felt that bad in my life— grief mixed with a huge caffeine upper is not a great combo.

Anyway, I pulled onto my street in front of the white colonial, completely wrung out from trying not to cry all day through class and a musical performance at the Van Andel Arena. After the comfort of seeing the first maple tree on my street and passing the yellow bungalow on the corner, my vision focused on my two-track driveway... And there he was. He was just leaving. My heart heaved forward in my chest; I tried as hard as I could not to act upset. He was visibly upset though, which surprised me...I was holding out hope he would change his mind. And I held out hope for months. I never gave him the satisfaction of knowing that though. But think of this, Ladies: I had FINALLY left the Lug. I had dated a gazillion Carloses in and among trying to leave the Lug. No one ever got me past him...except for Stephano. That's why I thought Stephano HAD TO BE the Good Knight. Have I mentioned I was thirty-three and I wanted kids? It was one of the most upsetting sick feelings I've ever had, watching my last chance get in his car and drive down the road.

Now: whew, by the way, there is a NOW, which means that life, does in fact, go on. Time changes. Hurt scabs over. Life dictates a new order of things. After some time, I figured out it wasn't really Stephano I was grieving. Cole had been right. Let's face it: Stephano was as intellectual as a box of rocks. Nice? For sure! Polite? Absolutely! But aware of grown-up issues with a propensity for life-long learning?... Not so much.

And of course he was way too immature. I'm sure he grew up eventually, but we just weren't in the same place in the same season. Cole insisted Stephano would be the guy with the beer gut sitting on the couch watching ESPN when he was forty and unemployed. I figured Cole was going a little too far, but he was correct in his discernment that, had I stayed with Stephano, I would have been ultimately unhappy. And fate was right to have taken the break-up out my hands and convince Stephano to end it, because my biological clock and lonely spirit would not have done it. It had to happen the way that it did. And if you're asking me to weigh out which of the deep pains in my life I now fall on my knees in gratitude for and regard as a blessing in disguise? This is it.

The Lug break-up hurt too, don't get me wrong. But it was so yucked up by the end, I knew there was no fixing it in spite of any love that was left. With Stephano it had been sudden, beautiful, lovely, welcoming and disarming. Did I mention his family?? In short—there had been more love and not so much yuck, so the pain of it leaving me felt way more sad and cutting.

So, Stephano became Rico Suavè.

For the record, [and one does need to keep a record or keep some type of "score" if you will, since there were so so so many bachelors on this show...]. But anyway, Cole with his cool and along with his discernment disliked the Lug OF COURSE, and he disliked Rico Suavè too. He liked Skip, but I didn't. He never met Carlose because it was one date, and he never met Nate either, even though I dated Nate for two months. But after the Christmas cookie/wine glass incident, I decided it wasn't worth bringing him around my family, *especially* Cole. Strangely, even though I wasn't personally "attracted to him," Cole liked Burk. Cole thought Burk was cool. It was weird to me: the Master of Cool thinks the redhead is cool. Huh.

Ten:
It's All Dante's Inferno, Hot Wind!

Funny how things change just like that. Six months prior I thought I was getting married to Stephano. Steph's entrance into my life was romantic and unexpected; he was NOT a product of the APB that had been issued a year or so earlier, but a real happenstance. Given this, I thought for sure he had to be the one, especially after seven years and two broken engagements with the Lug. I was contemplating this with eyes swollen almost shut from crying. In fact, they were so swollen and sore that I was having a difficult time reading *Twelfth Night* for English 342, so now I was crying about not being able to read my homework and what a sorry loner I was now and I'll never be able to do my homework which means I'll never get my teaching degree and I'm bound to be, therefore, broke and single forever, so why even try...

Mustering the courage and self-discipline to go downstairs and get an ice pack to reduce the swelling, I heard the phone ringing. I momentarily abandoned the ice pack and rushed to the phone hoping it was Stephano. I grabbed the handset and saw that it was Jeannine and answered, "Hi Darlin'. How ya doin'? I mean...I know you still feel sucky so it's a dumb question, but I'm still letting you know I'm thinking about you."

"Thanks Sweets," I whimpered back. And I truly was thankful because talk about a real life problem, Jeannine was on bed rest with her pregnancy while having to take steroids to avoid premature labor. She'd already spent weeks in the hospital because my niece tried to be born when she was a 24-week fetus. Jeannine was now beginning her seventh month of pregnancy and unable to go anywhere or do anything. Jeannine's call jerked me out of my own obsession with myself and my own needs. That was the moment I chose to go from devastated to just plain old blue. Seriously, it had been two weeks and I'm still crying until my eyes are swollen shut? I couldn't even stand to be around myself over the mere selfishness of it.

Eleven:
Standing Up

At some point Kids, we've got to stand back up. Who is going to pull us up? I kept thinking I needed some one else to do it, but the only person who could really do it was me. Sure, I had great friends who had been in it with me. My Mom especially, always saw the "good" in every situation to an annoying point of view.

"It's okay that you had to put the dog down—you were too busy to take care of him anyway."

"It's okay that Stephano broke up with you because he wasn't the right guy for you anyway." [Really mother? That's what you said after the last three break ups. Do you, does *anybody* think there is a right guy for Robyn at this point??] And my most recent favorite, "It's okay that Jeannine was demoted at work because she won't have time once the baby comes anyway." Gees, Mom. We're only sixty-five days away from the twenty-first century. Women work with babies now. Jeannine can do whatever she wants.

I knew my Mom probably understood this, but I had to have these verbal responses in my own head to her "fix it" comments, or I would self-destruct while nodding a knowing smile at each of these choice words of wisdom. However, if I were to look past her annoying comments for a minute [and for just *one minute*, because who could ignore these remarks altogether...], there was one element in my Mother's perceptions I saw as a tidbit of truth, which is that there is more than one way to looks at things. So, if I just took that idea and tried to choose to see the value of what I actually did have, maybe I could get through each day without dry heaving or puking. We'll see.

I thanked Jeannine for calling and told her I was "hanging in there," pretending my eyes weren't little slits because, as I mentioned, I was a tad bit ashamed of myself, given her present circumstances. It's true: things can always be worse. I rolled this around in my brain for awhile. Hmmmmm. What if I WAS married and finally became pregnant with that baby I so badly wanted and there was a good chance every single day I may not carry to term? What if I was dealing with THAT? So Jeannine is married and unlonely—it doesn't mean she isn't scared or sad or disappointed because she imagined her life circumstances would be different than they were. It's like when we see the skinny girl for example, and we assume her life is absolutely perfect because she's skinny. We view the skinny girl through this one filter, when the truth is nothing is ever that simple, right? We don't even realize there could be extenuating circumstances. And even if the circumstances have nothing to do with her skinniness, maybe she has some other tragedy. Our brains too often see someone from a distance and make a judgment call based on what is on the surface. But maybe the skinny girl is losing her house because she lost her job—maybe she's a single mom who hasn't seen her kids' dad for a decade. Maybe there's an unhappy marriage or worse, a controlling abusive spouse. Who knows? Who ever knows? Hmmmm.

So, I began to take stock of my situation: let's see here, what can I possibly cobble together out of this life? Okay, so I'm thirty-three. Well—I have this little house that I love (and I did love it even though it had a window problem, a roof problem, a basement problem, and an electrical problem). It was the cutest, most quaint adorable little house a single girl could own. And even though I had HORRIBLE roommates

[...except for Jenny, the first one who I sadly didn't get for very long], one after the other to be able to afford it, it was still the cutest house ever. It was a happy house; this happy house was my friend and I loved coming home to it.

Let's see....what else? Well, there's this chance at a second career to become a teacher. Hey!! Maybe I'm NOT going to have my own kids: just maybe there is a plan—maybe I'm meant to be freed up from parenting so I can love on somebody else's kids!

The lights of freedom began to click on in my mind—I have SO much. My life is full of muchness. And with that, I began to ease out of the grieving part of Stephano's exit. Remember how I had already kind of figured out that it wasn't Stephano himself that was the main source of the pain, it was what his departure symbolized? The chance to be married and be a mom? That's what I had really been grieving. That's why my eyes were swollen shut. That's why my body ached and I felt desperate to be unlonely. But now, that I saw there could be another purpose for my life with teaching, it took some pressure off from my reproductive organs and therefore my heart.

Don't get me wrong, I still wanted to get married and have a companion for life and have a child of my own, but: there is more than one way to do things. Let's say for example that I didn't meet my husband until I was..ahem...choke...gasp...fuh fuh fuh—FORTY. What if I was forty? Hmmmm. Well, the chances of having a baby at forty are lower than at say....twenty-five. So, maybe I could adopt a baby! Or I could, if the circumstances were correct, adopt a baby as single woman, maybe... The world was changing and beginning to open up to other possibilities.

And as a sidebar and for the record, it has been a proverb I've lived by ever since, that there is absolutely more than one way to accomplish things or view my circumstances. One of the reasons I'd been in so much pain for so long is because I had planned my own life out and when circumstances came along that did not match my own plan, it totally flipped me out. Uvvvve COURSE there's more than one way. But as I said, I lived like I didn't have choices or more than one path to happiness. My life was a perfect example of circumstances not working out as planned and therefore having to figure out how to do it a different way: I was thirty-three and changing careers. I was learning to adore Literature and Writing. Ten years prior in 1989, I was a professional musician—you could never have suggested I would do anything else then; there was no talking to me about it. And yet, here I was in 1999 going back to school—not nearly as many people were in colleges at a non-traditional age then, as have been in recent years. I was the oldest student in every class. Who cares?! There's more than one way. So now, when people around me are close-minded about methods or process and limit their own choices, I get really frustrated—who says we can't do it a different way? What committee said you have to have your career all picked out by the time you are 22? Who says you have to get married before 33? Or ever? Who says you can't have a baby or adopt a baby when you're 35? Who is the one we cave to when we can't have it the way we dreamt?

I had put incredible limits on my own life, People: it was my own fault that I was miserable. Yes, I did live in a small town. Yes, everyone gets married here when they are ten years younger than I was. Yes, I had a right to grieve when Stefano walked out because he took his family and friends with him, and I missed them *all* [...well, except for the drunken farting fraternity brothers]. My point is, yes, all these sadnesses happened; they were all true. But the idea that these circumstances destined me to be completely miserable and had therefore taken away my choices, was utterly ridiculous. I had chosen to be miserable. I had done it to myself. Everyone has the right to cry when someone leaves and walks out of their life. But if I chose to allow that to define me or weigh the amount of worth that I had? That's on me.

It's this simple: I learned that I no longer, could blame my present feelings about myself on my past. I could no longer use my past as an excuse to feel sorry for myself or to justify unhealthy behaviors [... behaviors, like staying with a man who treated me like shit for seven years because I had no choices. Or behaviors such as living my life like everything was about me, given the obsession I'd had with my loneliness and the distraction of wondering what it said about me that I was alone]. My poor friends and family: if they had a buck for every time they heard me say that out loud, "what does it say about me?" Gak. Puke. Yuck. Ick. I had worn my singleness around my shoulders like a shroud of grieving black.

The kick in my step was back. My heart was still sad from Stephano. And the Lug. And Burk a little too, 'cause I'd really liked him, and he, out of all them was the most like someone I could see myself with. Yet I'd thrown him away for the Lug too and did consider it a terrible waste. But I no longer wore my pain like I was entitled to it. I decided it was something I was allowed to feel but it would no longer dictate my choices or decisions or attitudes.

Twelve:
Profundity and Prerogative

Speaking of choices and decisions after I'd dumped Burk to go back to the Lug, I was sitting on my living room sofa talking to Cate on the phone: Cate was my mentor—a life coach of sorts. Remember the VIP's from church I mentioned earlier? Cate was a VIP in my life. She was a wolf in sheep's clothing. I had asked her a year or so earlier if she'd be willing to get together on occasion to go over stuff in my life....kind of like a therapist I guess. I felt connected to her even though I didn't even know her very well. I knew enough to have observed that she was a discerning and evaluative person. Ya know how sometimes if you offer unsolicited advice it can come back to bite you and bite you hard? Yeh...don't tell people what to do unless they ask your opinion. Then feel free to be honest. Otherwise, shut. Your. Mouth. How do you think I know this???

Anywho, I had asked Cate's opinion regarding my spiritual journey, my circumstances and my choices and decisions, so we'd been meeting once every other week for coffee. She skipped the pleasantries in order to make the most of our time. Sometimes she went straight for the jugular. Sometimes it was hard, but it was always good.

So anyway, back to my living room sofa that I was sitting on the edge of, bent over at the waist and staring into the rug; as I mentioned,

I was talking to Cate on the phone that day and she told me that she'd run into Burk at church a few times. She asked me, "Why did you stop dating him? He seems great."

"I da know Catie—I just wasn't attracted to him physically."

"Whut? Really?!"

"Yeh....why?"

"Robbi, I wouldn't go around telling people that you're not '*attracted to*' Burk because someday you might marry him." Before waiting for my response, she'd said this and it made my blood run cold. I still remember how many white specs of yarn were woven into the minuscule place on the rug beneath my feet—it was where I had focused my sight during our conversation: three. Three specs of white yarn.

My blood indeed felt chilly. But only for a second. I pushed it out of my mind. It's just that when Cate talked like that, she was usually never wrong. But just in case, I decided to not go around telling any more people I wasn't "attracted to" Burk or anyone else for that matter. I guess it is a girl's prerogative to change her mind and I'm pretty sure that's what she meant.

Thirteen:
Behind the Red Velvet Curtain

Behind the red velvet curtain there once was girl who believed she had no choices which, of course, is why she was behind the red velvet curtain in the first place. She was fraught with a crunchy hairdo so big, the sides looked as if she would take off. She was wearing a dress that was never meant to sit down in and high heels that were not designed to walk in. She was proud (or rather, thought she was supposed to be proud...) of her taped-up-pushed-out chest.

This girl was actually willing to put on a swimsuit while wearing those same high heels, stand in front of a panel of [mostly] men, and turn around for them in a perfect pivot in order that they be able to *judge* her physical fitness. Er...the category of "Physical Fitness" is what they call it now. Back then though, they called it what it was: the swimsuit competition. This girl was adorned in fake eye-lashes, the kind that Cruella de Vil peeled off at the end of each day, and was sporting orange skin. That's right: her skin was ORANGE. Tanning lotions weren't so good then. But it was okay really, because every girl had orange skin. She, along with all of them, looked like a bunch of skinny Halloween pumpkins, grinning through their over-smiled fixations and smelled like a herd of cows.

This girl was so uninformed about who she actually was, she thought she had to take her clothes off for approval! Okay, that's not exactly true. But she justified it as being "a small inconvenience she disliked and could put up with, for the greater good of 'exposure,'" no pun intended. She was a professional vocalist (and well, still kind of is—but isn't trying to make a living doing it anymore). It's difficult to make a go of a career in music if you don't live in one of the big three: LA, New York, or Nashville. Sure there are a lot of great cities known for their music, but if *this girl* wanted an honest chance, she needed to give herself a go of it in a place that had the most chances. Grand Haven, Michigan wasn't it. This girl reasoned out that pageantry was an avenue to a career in professional music that was a little closer to home than LA.

My Mom eventually surmised that "God gave Robyn the stage presence and vocal talent to be a career artist, but He didn't give her the personality." She meant that I was a homebody, so the idea that I would be happy living out of hotel rooms and dragging my butt from city to city every night, 50 weeks per year wouldn't fly. Yet, because that's what it takes to achieve and maintain a music career, especially when you're young in it, this was the inevitable lifestyle—it's not really for those who like to be home... But anyway, I didn't know that about myself yet and I'm fairly certain she didn't know it about me yet either, which is why she supported my pageantry efforts.

Some girls compete in their local pageant growing up and it's just one of the many, in a collection of, racked-up adolescent experiences. But I? Oh, I made a career out of it. I competed in eight local pageants over the course of five years. I competed at the State level three times. Heeeeeerrrrrrreeeeee's what I thought, or at least told myself, as I'd had reasoned it out justifying it: since talent was fifty percent of the final score, I had a good chance to win the state pageant and go on to Nationals. Even girls at Nationals who make the top ten, yet who don't necessarily win, get television exposure. There are many talent scouts and record label execs who attend these events and watch them for just that! I figured it wasn't a bad route to a record deal.

But, I just didn't want to admit it was a bad route. Let's see, here's what bugged me about pageantry: the nasty, crappy (and I mean CRAPPY) girls, the constancy of comparing oneself, particularly body size to the others, constantly sizing up your "talent" against the others or checking to see if your gown was as pretty as the other girls'; this comparison thing was a losing proposition because there was always an "other girl" who had a prettier dress, whiter teeth, or who was more "physically fit." And I didn't like either, what these unfortunate aspects of constant comparison caused in me, including jealousy, eating disorders, shame, and fear. We ALL had aspects of ALL of these non-attributes. Can you imagine if one pageant girl at one place in time were honest about one detail regarding pageant involvement?

Hypothetical David Letterman Interview

"So Taryn, How do you get your swimsuits to stay down and not ride up while you're walking in those 4-inch heels?"

"Thanks for asking Mr. Letterman. We actually use a spray product called 'Firm Grip.'"

"Fuh fuuhhirrrrm GaahRippp?" [Dave's forehead is heightened, exposing all present horizontal wrinkles.]

"Yes, it's actually a product used by tennis players to keep their rackets from falling out of their hands when they get sweaty during match play."

Dave's eyebrows rising up on his forehead again and his eyes opening up as big as hubcaps: "You spray that...somewhere?"

"Why yes Mr. Letterman! We take turns bending over: after we have our suits on, we hike them up as if they were a great big thick thong and spray the exposed skin. Then we *carefully* pull the swimsuit down over the sticky skin and whalah! Swimsuit firmly in place!"

Dave staring: "So...so...[audience laughing nervously in awkward sporadic laughs]...does it ever get....stuck in the wrong...spot?"

Can you imagine this interview? Ha! I can't either because no one ever tells you any of the true stuff. The truth is that anything you've ever imagined to be true about pageantry most-probably is! How about this one:

The Tonight Show With Jay Leno

"So Emily, what do you do for fun?"

"Thanks for asking Mr. Leno: on Saturday nights," head shifting left to right to make sure no one but Jay and the studio audience are listening, "I put on my sweat pants and sit on the couch for a date with my..my...food. I *might* eat a 2 pound bag of peanut M&M's, a 1/2 gallon of ice cream—I'll eat a full gallon but instead I save room for the pizza. Yes, I follow up ice cream with an entire pizza. Then, when no one is looking, I go throw it all up. And then? Well, then I lay on my bed and cry because there's a chance I didn't get it all up and my body will actually process some of that fat and sugar you know, so then I am upset because I'll gain some weight, you see??! Anyway, what do you do for fun Mr. Leno??"

I get your discomfort—this second one isn't funny like the David Letterman interview, but it goes to my point that everything you can possibly imagine you've ever suspected could be true about pageantry most probably is, and it's the part that no one tells you.

So, of course I knew these dreadful things were going on and although I didn't like to think about it much, deep inside of me I knew pageantry wasn't actually going to work as a strategy in career advancement for my music. Don't get me wrong; I tried to win—I trained, I studied, I listened, I observed, I went to vocal lessons, and walking lessons, and the best dress shop, which? Was shockingly in St. Joseph, Michigan... St. Joe was a Michigan town actually more known for its crime rate than anything else, so why the best pageant-gown store in the state was in this town, I'll never know.

If I'd throw myself any type of a bone for any of the experience, I would say that I honestly was one of the very few nice girls: I never tried to slash a dress—I won my crown [okay...."Crow-NS") fair and square. And I won several of them fair and square with my sequins, firm grip, support hose (before there were Spanx, there were JC Penney support hose and once they were on you, you could not breathe) and my duct-taped boobs.

Ladies hear me: the truth is, there were all kinds of good attributes I brought to pageants and took out of them. But when it was all said and done, what had I really gained? I was still the same great vocalist I had been going in. Pageants didn't give me that. Hard work and a gazillion hours of voice lessons had. I had the same awesome interview skills I'd always had (which helped me get the first teaching job I interviewed for later on). The point Gals, is that I didn't need THAT vehicle to prove I was good at stuff. Here we all are with our gifts, talents and offerings that we can express to the world around us. I unnecessarily attached, support hose, duct tape, Vaseline'd teeth, and Final Net to mine. I put myself in a box. I let the world define me within the confines of that box. Oh, I told myself alright that it was a means to an end but ...I never *really* believed that the end justified the means. I suspected I didn't believe it at least, and when it was over? I had nothing extra to show for my music career. What I did have were insecurities, self-doubt, eating disorders and only one or two good friends.

Enter Denaya: she was not one of those friends. Nope. Denaya was a girl quite frankly who had no business being in pageants anyway.

Everything about her was manufactured. I'm not saying I was trying to be any less fake but at LEAST I *could* sing. Denaya began competing in pageants with the "dramatic monologue" which is a talent that contestants try when they don't have one that can be performed in 2 minutes and 40 seconds. The talent competition works out for women who can sing, or dance, play an instrument or twirl the baton. [I'll get to the baton-twirler in a second!] But so Denaya anyway, had eventually moved out of dramatic monologue into singing and Dudettes? It was not good.

Now try to remember that this was before American Idol and endless montages of people performing badly in frame-to-frame looping. If you were bad at Miss Michigan, you stood out. 'Cause as fake as all these sisters were, they WERE all pretty—they were ALL talented—they were ALL beautiful. Except Denaya. She was kind of clunky, like Imogene Herdman from The *Greatest Christmas Pageant Ever*, but just cleaned up a little on the outside. And I have to honestly say that if Denaya had known she sucked, then perhaps I would have been more compassionate. But she was an evil, twisted, snotty, gossipy, triangulating witch. Oh she'd call up the director and make up something about you that wasn't true and you'd find out about it through someone who overheard the director talking to another person, so then you'd get ticked off and call up the director and ask, "is this true" and the director would hmmm and haw and finally come out with it and you'd get even more ticked, all the while begging the director to believe your side of it. It was righteously unhealthy. This is just one example of the thirty-seven incidents I could tell you that the lovely Denaya caused over her lustrous pageant career.

But I do have to give her this: although she wasn't exactly talented or nice or fun or generous, or attractive for that matter, she was SMART. And that is why she won so many locals and also competed at State three times. There's a system, and she figured out how to grease the skids. None of it was authentic and yet, her résumé ended up showing the same earnings as mine.

So, it just goes to show that in an environment as false as pageantry, if you are disliked for being of all things...fake....it's sayin' somethin' about the level of fake, ya know what I mean??? We were all trying so hard to be something we weren't, but Denaya put a special definition to it and come to think of it, I think it was her talent.

So she was not one of the friends I took out of the experience. She was a person I wanted to forget I'd ever met. Sharon however, was a friend I liked. She was a surprise. She was tall and willowy and best of all, sincere. But the coolest thing about her was that she twirled the baton: she twirled three batons in the air at once, juggling them as they were spinning horizontally and wait for it....while they were on FIRE. She always won the talent competition as she should have. It was redonkulously nutso cool and I never got tired of watching her perform or practice that. But she was shockingly humble about it and I saw in her a kindred spirit. "Here's someone," I thought "who is using this as a means to an end too, but doesn't truthfully belong here either." I saw into her and she saw into me. So although we were competing for the same titles at the same time, I was never sad when she beat me. I was happy for her. She managed to stay a person I looked forward to seeing, instead of becoming a person I was afraid of, and we respected each other.

I realize there are many-a-gal who went through the pageant world, did well by it and it by them. Gretchen Carlson, Miss America 1989, is a good example of what I mean—she's worked as a national television journalist. She was an exquisite violinist and could have gone onto play in the philharmonic. She was sure of herself and won Miss America after having competed in only one local pageant, and one state pageant, Miss Minnesota. That's it. She wasn't in it quite long enough to be skewed by it perhaps??

Pageants aren't *all* bad, if I'd perhaps just done it once like Ms.

Carlson. What was bad for me was that I did it for too long and for the wrong reasons: acceptance and approval. In the beginning, as I mentioned, I told myself it was about the musical opportunities it could open up, but by the end it had taken on a life of need of its own. Oh I was approved of by the locals in my town alright—they treated me like a celebrity (which I was not, but which I ate up...until I had ridden in my seventh parade of the season: the Holland Tulip Time Festival Parade. Did you know that the Holland Tulip Time Festival parade is the second longest parade in the nation, second only to the Tournament of Roses Parade? Let me tell ya girls...when you're waving in freezing rain on a float for 5 hours and you're wearing nothing more than a sequined slip? The celebrity wears off REAL fast.) And one wonders how I could look back at that season and shake my head? Jiminy Christmas.

For five years I did duct tape, Vaseline, Firm Grip, Final Net, back-combing, teasing and the fervent sucking in of my gut, while teetering around in teetery-tottery spiky heels and it was during this season that I met the Lug. It is not surprising then perhaps, why I didn't have the self-respect to tell him to get lost after the first time he cheated.

Fourteen:
G. Louise, Profits & Loss, and Individually Indigent

After my fledgeling career as a beauty queen came to a screeching halt due to the age limit (and thank God there was an age limit, right, or I may have kept doing it for a decade or two...) and, also given my otherwise-valuable but not-count-on-able music career, there was an intense push by the Lug for me to "legitimize" myself. He didn't want to be married to an artist I guess—it seemed that my maybe-music vocation wasn't enough for his ego. So, he suggested that I do something slightly less "non sequitur" than simply consider myself a musician.

Okay, so let me get this straight, Lug: you're asking me to change my career, but really what you want is for me to change my identity. Lug, allow me to explain my angst: perhaps you've failed to pick up the facts in the two years we've been dating. Let's see, I've studied voice professionally since the age of twelve, and by the time I was twelve, I'd already performed in gatherings with over a thousand in attendance. My Dad was a gospel hymn-sing music leader—remember that Lug? And, he trusted my musical gifts so much, he put me up in front of people when I was six, not just to be cute but to actually give a serious thought-provoking performance, remember? And oh yeh Lug, I studied music through college, went to Nashville and recorded an entire record album of thirteen songs, four of them originals [which admittedly bombed.... but it was still an enormous accomplishment]. And then I went the route of pageantry to try to find some professional recognition of musical opportunity and am still hoping to get a record deal Lug. But, I'll just take all twenty-six years of my life's work, commitment, study and experience, and place it in shoebox up on a shelf all the way in the back of the closet, right up there next to the box which contains my high school science tests! In fact, if it makes YOU feel better Lug, I'll just trash my identity as a musician altogether without keeping it as a hobby even, and put it out with the morning garbage. Oh, what was that? You said I shouldn't feel like it should be trashed, but recycled rather? No! Don't worry Lug—it's all about you! Even my identity is going in the trash can, not the recycling bin. I am happy to just set all of that aside because you think I should.

Sarcastic ranting aside, conversations like these actually took place, the sarcasm part remaining inside my head however. No matter though, I was moving on because the Lug said so. Subsequently, the summer I'd lost Miss Michigan for the last and final time, I began looking in the newspaper for something less "non-sequitur" and otherwise more legitimate. I had worked some retail in the past and loved fashion, so veered towards looking at jobs for help needed in clothing shops. I looked at department stores too, but I wanted an experience with more personal intent and contact with customers than some vast dress department, or a one-stop shopping establishment offered; I was a people person. And also, I figured if I was going to work every Friday night and Saturdays for minimum wage, I thought that I wanted it to be in a more glamorous atmosphere than dog toys and breakfast cereals merchandized across the aisle from one another. When you're new in retail, you have to work weekends. The dream schedule of working Monday through Friday from eight to five doesn't exist in retail for those low in seniority. So, I searched in a fervent manner for something besides Hudson's at the mall or Walmart.

Needless to say the Lug wasn't thrilled about this retail thing: he wanted me to be an engineer or a business executive, claiming if retail was "all I did," then I wouldn't have enough to talk with him about, or enough to keep myself "interesting." But ya know what? In spite of his nerve, even he knew his pushing had its limits. We were still at the point in the relationship when he was hot for me, so I think his eventual prudence decided it would be smart to back-off the business executive/engineer pressure, out of concern that I might run away to Nashville if he kept on. [And I mean *really*...I had a college degree consisting of liberal arts sciences, music theory/performance training, Biblical Study and content seminars, business classes and also, some environmental science thrown in there for good measure. I called this a "mutt degree" because it had a little bit of everything, but specialized in well....nothing exactly. So Lug, you want me to become an engineer? For a smart guy, he hadn't bothered to check the qualification facts that such a vocation required.]

However: I did feel somewhat qualified to work in retail, not just because of my fashion passion, but also I was from a business/sales family, which is its own kind of school in teaching the ethics of hard work combined with profits and loss. You might have heard of this fine institution known as, "The School of Hard Knocks." Although I was unsure about how to frame it on my resume', I knew it counted. For example, I learned that a good Dutch business man does not pay an employee to clean his warehouse on Saturdays. Nor does he pay for electricity during said cleaning. Instead, he has his underage children do it for free of course! Not only that, but he has them do it for free in the dark.

"Cole, grab this push broom!"

"Robbi, here's the 409. Clean the Hi-Low! Make it sparkle!"

"Ah, Jef? You come over here and work with me moving these boxes...." and "...try not to break anything," he added with caution, due to Jef's tendency to be a little awkward and heavy-handed. There were many-a-Saturday spent in a dusty cement-floored warehouse, where it was so dark, it was like a basement without any windows. To save money, my Dad would bring flashlights and crack open one of the loading-dock garage doors (out of the ten available). His prudent calculator suggested that the mere firing up of the mains for a little Saturday cleaning would cost too many electrical dollars. There was a budget for goodness sake! Overhead lighting on Saturday exceeds that budget! My mother always said that my Dad never paid a dollar more for anything than he had to, which at first just seems like common sense. But my Daddy redefined what "had to/having to" meant. His children didn't *have to* be able to see, right, in order to help clean?!

Speaking of my mother, she would nervously pace during these incidences, doing her 1970's best to maintain her reputation as a non-bossy wife. She was no wallflower let me tell you, in spite of the fact that she looked the wallflower part given her bouffant hair, pleated skirt and proper hand gloves. But she walked a fine line between being a woman who came of age during the women's movement, combined with the dynamic of marrying a man a generation older than herself. But she had her limits too—When she just couldn't take it anymore, an exasperation would pour out of her: "JACK!!! This is unacceptable!" However, Jack was not persuaded.

There was another time that best explains my father's feelings on the topics of Profits, Loss and Work-Ethic: my job as a "ranch-hand" at Grace Youth Camp. GYC, as it was otherwise known, was a 501c3 organization that my father had founded twenty years or more prior, with which he remained a ranking board member. I was crazy into riding horses by the time I was sixteen with an unquelled enthusiasm, so I begged my Dad for a job teaching horsemanship at summer camp. Although he was not the acting director, he finagled me a "position." This turned out to be rather disappointing however, because it was not the teaching position I felt was due my esteemed self. See, as with any career, one has to start "in the mailroom" so to speak. Well, the mailroom at a ranch? Can you guess? Yep, it has to do with lots and lots of horse CRAP. So instead of working with campers and leading trail rides, I shoveled horse shit all day. I'm not exaggerating for the sake of a clever point here. It was:

all day.

All day, I pushed a wheelbarrow through a dust-bowl ridden field, scooped all of the manure from twenty eliminating horses into the wheel barrel, wheeled it back across the field and dumped it in a huge pile. It was a hot, fly-biting, terrible job so you can imagine when pay day came, I was ready to get some jing and *spend* some jing! But alas, my payday envelope was empty, except for a note of thanks mentioning the organization's appreciation for "my service" from some committee at the front office.

I dialed my Dad from a pay phone in Mears, Michigan ['couldn't risk it from the camp's free desk phone, since it was on a party line and someone may overhear...] at his business office in Grand Rapids: "Dad?! There was....umm...no money in my 'paycheck' envelope!"

"Right."

"But Dad, the other employes my age, including counselors and kitchen staff are getting paid."

"Listen here Young Lady!—No daughter of mine is taking a dollar out of that camp. That camp exists due to the sweat of my brow and the callouses on my hands. [He was right about that—Grace Youth Camp had a stockpile of sweat equity in it.] Therefore, you can eat in the dining hall and stay in the lodge, but more compensation than THAT?! No way!" Clearing his throat, I sensed he realized his own intensity because he gathered himself a little and finished with, " Uhhh... consider this an internship...of sorts...."

Ahhhhhh, I had no choice but to do so or go home. At least my father was raising a chic who wasn't a quitter. I sucked it up and stayed for six more weeks and no, it didn't get any better until the next summer when I was promoted slightly to leading trail rides and direct horse care. I suspect this promotion had to do with a closed-door meeting by my mother, who again reiterated her feelings regarding children working in hazardous environments, expressing that the circumstances were "unacceptable." Promotion or no promotion though, it was still for no pay!

Yet about ten years later as I endeavored to find a career other than professional music, I looked back at these experiences (and many others like them) as the building blocks of toughness my father said that I should, so although my formal education provided little in the way of business management, maybe I could impress a retailer with my life experience.

One day I ran into an old friend who told me that the owner of G. Louise was looking for a new manager for her beautiful, quaint and upscale boutique in downtown Grand Haven. I was intrigued and excitedly curious, because I'd stopped in there a few times in the past to look for some outfits for special-occasion events. So I called the owner and she agreed to meet me for coffee to discuss the opportunity. I thought carefully that I should not include mention of the job depicting my excellent horse-crap scooping skills on the résumé and also omitted the underage warehouse cleaning as well.

Yep. That's right. The letter "G" followed by a period, followed by the lovely name "Louise." G. Louise was an upscale boutique to match its name in downtown Grand Haven. The founder auspiciously named it G. Louise because her mother's name was Louise, and her mother's best friend's name was ALSO Louise. These two lovely Louises called each other at 5 pm every Saturday no matter where either of them happened to be in the world—they never missed a week, in spite of the fact that one could be in Belgium and the other could be in Panama [Belgium and Panama being mere examples of the momentary Timbuktu destinations where these Louises might happen to be.] And yet, no matter what side of the conversation you sat on, you would hear "Gee Louise, You don't say!"... this and "Gee Louise, Isn't that somethin'?!" that. So, when one of the Louise's ambitious daughter opened her boutique, she named it G. Louise in homage to her mother and friend's weekly assemblage.

And so I met Fancy Francie. Now before you accuse me of plagiarism, let me just tell you that before there ever existed a prolific series of children's books about a cute little red head named "Fancy Nancy," there was an esteemed, beautiful creature named Francine Reegland. She did go by "Francie" with some her close friends, but the "fancy" part was just my private nickname for her. She was regal and fancy and classy and smart and it just fit her. When I met her for coffee that day, I was impressed by what made this woman so unique: she was the perfect combination of sophistication and elegance, combined with business acumen and academic smarts. Francie was a class act. Her boutique was actually her "hobby," she explained as she had another career directing an area nonprofit organization. She called her work there, her "other life."

"In my other life, I have to wear these business suits and so that's why I carry some here at G. Louise because I know women want to look classy even when they need to be professional, but I also love outfitting women in special occasion clothes or a hip trouser and blouse. Hiring you is going to be great for the store, but we need to remember that the merchandise cannot get 'too young' just because you're young; otherwise my trusted customer base will find another boutique to patronize." She raised an eyebrow and stared over her coffee cup: after a brief pause, she added, "It's simple, really: women over forty generally have more money to spend on clothes. I cater to *them.*"

I knew what she meant: Keep it classy—no mini skirts—no acid wash denim—no see through mesh Madonna crap—No fishnet stockings—no hair bows the size of a Lake Michigan trout. Plunging necklines? Yes, as long as there is adequate "support." Fitted funky blouses? Of course...but this is classier if it remains long-sleeved. Backless dresses? Heck yeh, but then the skirt on it has to be long to limit the sexiness—my older clientele are not comfortable going around looking like "sluts." Even the word "sluts" rolled off her tongue as if she were an esteemed English professor teaching it like it was a vocabulary word. Okay—I think I've got it Francine! Class, not trash. I'm in.

G. Louise was as beautiful as Fancy Francie. It was in the lower space of a building more than a hundred years old and was on a popular block of the busiest street in downtown Grand Haven, right across the street from Fortinos General Store. The front windows had a stage built into them and were positioned on either side of the French-style front doors. The entire space was a floor-to-ceiling two-story room. The building was painted forest green and Francie had black lacquer painted on all of the trim. It was regal but in a retro cool way—not in a Pretty-Women-Rodeo-Drive stuck up way. The floors were original wood planks that were high-glossed and the walls were original brick. It was a lovely environment in which to spend everyday, the scent of slow-roasted, shell-on peanuts from Fortinos across the street, wafting in every so often.

But here's the thing: if we set this beautiful description aside, I have a fair question: have you ever tired to make money working retail? I'm not asking if you can make enough to pay the bills. You probably can. I'm asking if you think you can actually make money, like....get ahead? The beautiful Fancy Francie not withstanding, most employed retail sufferers know that you make minimum wage until you work your way up to earning commission, and if you're faithful and a little lucky, you can make some decent jing at the management level. The problem is there's more of a need in retail sales than there is in retail management and so although I was faithful, I wasn't very lucky. Yes, Francie made me the manager, and it did a lot for my self-esteem because it was a real job with real responsibilities, not just a title. There was merchandising and marketing and the buying of inventory in Chicago and New York, the managing of employees and of course, direct work with customers. The position was true to its description.

However, Fancy Francie couldn't pay me more than she could afford because she was *also* trying to make money since she of course owned the business and all. So as great as the job and the position were, the pay was exactly what it would have been, whether I'd worked for any other retail store, which? Was ...not so great. You retailers totally get what I'm saying, right? Like this talk of raising the minimum wage to over twenty bucks an hour makes you want to cry a lake, right? Regardless of individual political leanings, small business folks freak out about it because of this simple truth: Ya can't squeeze blood out of a turnip. Profound, right? There is sadly, no money tree out back. How do you think I know this?

Because one day, about six months after my employment with her began, Fancy Francie came over to the store on her lunch break (she usually came in from 3-6, after her work at the Nonprofit was finished for the day). She walked over to the front counter as I was finishing up with a customer. Once the satisfied shopper exited with her shopping bags, Francine looked at me with one eyebrow ever-so-slightly higher than the other, her lip tight on one side where I thought I could tell she'd chewed off a little of her bronze lipstick and said this: "Robyn. I want to sell the store." My mouth dropped open. BOTH of *my eyebrows* were raised now.

"Why?! I love it here—...ya...YOU love it here! You're soooo good at this—" I stammered and continued to stammer out similar utterances. Francine sighed.

"I just have too much on my plate. I've been doing this for six years, I like 'my other life' at the Nonprofit...and well...." She paused. I leaned in. I could tell she had a little more to say but was hesitating. I raised my eyebrows a little more to try to communicate that it was okay for her to be honest if she needed to be. She continued, "...and well....my marriage...is...well..uhh..." I jumped in, to save her from having to explain anymore.

"I understand." And I did, because although she didn't share very much, I had suspected there was trouble. She had never missed a chance to tell me how she felt about the Lug, his attitude and treatment of me. It was interesting really, because although she was a complete professional and almost aloof at times, she managed to skip the pleasantries on any given day to explain that I deserved a better man and that I should treat myself with more respect when it came to who I would marry. It was beginning to make sense now, her endeavors to cut through and get her feelings across in spite of the otherwise careful distance she maintained from anything too relational: she saw in me someone who didn't have to make the same mistakes that she had with a no-good knight. She'd married a World-Conquering type twenty-five years prior. He was a Great Knight: a war veteran, a physician, wealthy, popular and too handsome for his own good. All of these details from little bits of conversation gathered over the past six months came together in my head right then and there, and they equalled this conclusion. Therefore, my compassion exceeded my disappointment when I responded to her decision.

"What's next then??" I asked, "...you said you're 'selling,' not '*closing,*' correct?!" She simultaneously nodded and before she could say anymore I eeked out, "So, what does that mean for me? Will the next owner hire me?"

"Well actually," she said, "Here's what I came in here to ask you. Would you be interested in buying it? I am first offering it to you. I really want you to buy it."

So I did what any smart, logical, young business-yuppie of my generation would do: I bought the store. I reasoned that it was an opportunity to make more money than I would earn working for minimum wage for a different owner and this way, I would have *control!* That's right, People: you go to the bank, ya get a loan for about....ohhhh..a hundred thousand dollars or so when you're twenty-six years old, in order to purchase a business so you can make *more* money than you would have, than if you stayed working at minimum wage. Ay. Yi. Yi.

So a couple of guys walk into a bar. Kidding kidding kidding: work with me: A couple of guys walked into my store one day about a year later. By this time I was a permanent fixture on the floor of this recognizable boutique where "everybody knows your name." People I knew walked in to talk to me all of the time, figuring it more effective than the telephone because they knew they could corner me. I liked some aspects of this. I disliked some aspects of this. Like, sometimes I'd look up from the front counter and there was my Mom walking in with my hobbling Daddy. The stroke he'd had years before had left him with a gimpish limp but his grin never went away. So, there they'd come, this funny odd couple [doesn't everyone think their parents, if still married, are odd together?] asking me if I had dinner plans.

"Mom...you could have called..."

"Well yes, but we were in the neighborhood anyway," as if the ten mile drive from their home was a neighborhood location my father had limped over from. But she wasn't the only offender. Jef came in all the time:

"Hey Rob—can I get the 'family discount' for a gift for my friend, Trisha?" Sure Jef—*Really—I'll still make money if I give you twenty-five percent off since clearly I have NO overhead here?!* Oh, and then there was Karissa, my glamorous assistant who was asked out all of the time on the floor of the store. One day I'll never forget, she was standing in the middle of the store re-merchandizing a manikin. Her tall lithe frame was draped in Kenar black-crepe suiting, when a nice looking guy came in, walked right up to her and said, "Hey—I've been meaning to ask you out!"

Karissa stared at him. She did nothing. She said nothing. She had the perfect poker face.

This forced his next question, which was, "Soo...uhhh...will you go out with me?" Again, she looked straight at him with no expression. She didn't even blink.

"No," she said. That was it. He turned and left and I figured it served him right, since he cornered her at work like that. Karissa's ability to switch on a dime baffled me because she was otherwise outgoing, funny and from a huge family. There's a reason she worked in sales—she was great with people, but she knew when to hold 'em and she knew when to fold 'em. I guessed I should take a play from her book if I could manage it. So, G. Louise was a kind of stalking grounds of sorts I guess, which brings me back my story about the two guys who walked in.

It was Cole and his best friend, Bobby. They were covered from head to toe in engine grease, since they'd spent the morning installing boat engines. I looked at Cole and asked, "Ummm...Dude—what are doing here like that?"

"Like what?"

"Cole—you're wearing engine grease and you are standing four inches from a two-hundred dollar dress." Cole looked down at his own shirt and said,

"Oh—sorry—," and before I could say anything else, he winked at me and tilted his head to the right, gesturing towards Bobby. I read the look on Cole's face: it said, "Do. Not. Embarrass. Him." This was code for "It was Bobby's idea. He wanted to stop in here because we were in the neighborhood to get lunch..." (which I believed, because Cole and Bobby did often frequent the Pronto Pup hotdog stand around the corner). Funny how siblings can have an entire conversation with one another with facial expressions.

It had become clear for a while now that Bobby had a little crush on me. Looking back, I think it was Cole's idea to talk Bobby into having a crush on me in an attempt to do anything to get me away from the Lug. Whatevs. I didn't like Bobby that way because he'd been my brother's buddy for so long, it felt like I would be going out with a relative! Ick!

"Hey Cole, since you're here I need to talk to you about something real quick..." Bobby took the hint and said he'd meet Cole at the Pronto Pups' and smiled at me as he walked out. Cole called after him, "Yeh Dude—I'll meet you in a sec—" and before Cole could say anything I managed to squeeze in a plea for him to come help me the next day to set up for Sidewalk Sales. There were customers buzzing about, so I hoped the business of the moment would procure his quick agreement to assist me.

"Robbi, Bobby and I have to finish this boat! I don't have time to help with sidewalk sales!" He rolled his eyes in sarcasm as if it were some mamby pamby chosen activity I enjoyed to pass the time or something. I was annoyed. Grand Haven Sidewalk Sales was the event of the season for retailers: it was always about the second week of August where the downtown shops opened at 8:00 am instead of the usual 10:00, where the shop owners drastically reduced their prices on whatever merchandise was leftover from the feast of summer selling. It was now time to unload the old to have extra cash to purchase new merchandise and it was one crazy event. Racks upon racks of clothing/accessories had to be moved out onto the sidewalk. My girls could help me, but some of the display pieces were too heavy.

"Look Cole: I just need your brawn for thirty minutes. Can't you come in here tomorrow morning a half hour before you open, to help me move some furniture around??!"

"Rob—I was already going in 'early?!' Where's that boyfriend of yours—why can't *he* help you?" Cole had a point. The Lug was always busy with his work or his sailboat or buying grocery cereal with coupons or some such reason why he couldn't help me. I looked back at Cole admitting with my look he was right about the Lug's lame excuses.

"Fine," he said rolling his eyes again, "But you're taking Bobby too!"

"Fine. But I'm not agreeing to go on a date with him. Lug and I are exclusive." He smiled a sarcastic grin and came back with,

"Yeh, for the moment! It's only a matter of time…"

"Goodbye Cole." I glared at him. "I'll see you tomorrow morning at 7:00!" He turned and muttered something like "Yeh…yeh…" waving his arm over his shoulder as he turned around.

The next day, Cole and Bobby indeed showed up in an ungreasy fashion as I had required. We got it all moved out onto the street, my staff working to merchandise it as lovely as possible despite the sidewalk environment. I looked over and saw Karissa pick up a sundress and write an enormous "$15" on the price tag with a big red sharpie. The dress was originally $140 and had already been marked down to half price! "Ummmm—what are you doing? That could go down to half of half price, at the lowest, probably $35."

"It's ugly. It needs to go. It's been here since March and since it's now August? Well...that means it's ugly." She had a point.

At 8:00 a.m. sharp, security removed the ropes from around the four-block downtown area and scads of people came from all directions. It was already eighty-four degrees. There were pieces of tissue paper floating in the air while clothes were flying all over the place. I had one staff member ringing and bagging, one running around picking up everything that had been dropped on the ground or loosely tossed back onto a table that had slid off. I was running the fitting rooms, and another gal was out there on the periphery of our store's sidewalk area simply making sure no one shoplifted. By Noon, the total on the register showed three thousand dollars in sales which meant we'd sold a truckload of merchandise given the slashed prices. A fight broke out over a scarf between a mom pushing twins in a double stroller and a middle-aged woman:

"I saw it first!" the mom shouted.

"Kids these days!" retorted the middle-ager, suggesting the mother of twins was a kid. "It doesn't matter if *you saw it first,* I was touching it first!" The mom got a look on her face that said, "Did you just call me a kid???!" Then in an outrage, they both began to tug on it to the point where I thought they were going to rip it! The twins' mom won.

By four o'clock it was ninety-three degrees and I, hot, sticky, and exhausted was tired, frankly, of the customers begging for lower prices than the ones marked. Didn't they care that I was already losing gobs of money today? Yes, this sale was good for cash flow but not-so-much for the P&L statement! Exasperated, I emphatically expressed a resounding "NO" to the last lady who asked if I would consider "taking less for this belt?"

"NO!" I responded perhaps too loudly. Someone will pay five dollars for this!!! I can't let it go it for less than five because the original price was fifty!" [...Listen here Lady, in case you are unfamiliar with "Keystone Markup," it means that we as a store, had paid twenty-five dollars for the belt, so selling it for five bucks was already highway robbery. Oh, you want me to go down to four or three? For crying out loud, just take it for free Lady! I mean, we're not trying to do anything here like....*make a living!*]

So after three years, it became doggone apparent that I wasn't going to be able to beat the math with owning a fashion boutique in a beach town, where the local economy works on a feast versus famine principle. Retailers feast for three resort hot summer months and experience famine for the remaining nine when vacationers pack up and go home for the winter. Do you know how I knew this was apparent?

I could not afford to buy food.

I was hungry.

Being hungry got old.

Even though I knew the majority of the blame was not due to a lack of my talent, and did in fact belong at the feet of the economic reality in my town at the time, it wasn't enough comfort to get past the empty cupboards. The math simply didn't compute and so after several years of gerbil wheeling, I wanted off.

Some people say that everything happens for a reason. Well, I sort of believe that. Here's what I mean: I do think some outcomes are just inevitable because they are akin to the laws of gravity: for example, if you drop something, it will in fact, go down. Even if you drop something as delicate and light as a feather, it will still flutter to the ground, instead of hanging in the balance of space where you let go of it. So some decisions lead to poor outcomes because the outcomes are inevitable and therefore, preventable. My outcome with G. Louise was precalcuable, had I considered *all* of the facts and numbers. But I'd only considered one number which was the one associated with my yearning to be "legitimized" with a "real" career. It sounded good after all: "I'm a business owner." It made me feel strong to say that about myself when asked the inescapable question on outings with the Lug's business associates: "What do you do?" Answering them with "I'm a small business owner" sounded better than, "I'm a washed up pageant girl and a wanna be music star." I chose to go into that much debt because my ego mattered more than my bank account and it was an expensive lesson.

But let's say I were to have run ALL of the numbers and circumstances: like hey, it's a fashion boutique in a beach town where shopping and sales have a feast/famine economy and that will make things hard. I'm twenty-six. It's a hundred grand. That's a whole lot of money. The Coastguard Festival carnival-worker does not form my customer base, and he and others like him are downtown a LOT during our "feast" season. Fancy Francie owns this business yes, but it's not her livelihood, it's her hobby—a hobby she's passionate about and the passion shows, yes, but still...if it fails it won't bankrupt her. Perhaps I should pre-calculate buying this business based on these facts. Maybe this is not a good idea for an infamous-yet-trying-to-be gospel music singer.

But: I also believe that there is more than one way to view the financial mistake I'd made: it could be redeemed for its positive attributes too! What I mean is that if I had to do it over, I wouldn't have bought G. Louise because it was a whole bunch of debt, even after I sold it. 'Member I mentioned I had to move back in with my parents for a stint which, is why I didn't judge Nate at first? Yep. I spent ten months staying in my parents' guest room working to pay off the debt incurred by the sale of my business that didn't clear the loan. So yeh...it wasn't fun moving out of a cute condo on the waterfront channel (next door to a good taco stand I might add), selling much of what I owned and moving in with my parents at age twenty-nine. BUT, and there's a reason it's a big "but!" I *am* able to glean the following chicken scratches for the other side of my mistake: working for the beautiful Fancy Francie, the experience of business ownership which beefed up my résumé and helped me get my first teaching job six years later. Also, owning the store gave me a work ethic like nothing I'd ever experienced (even more than my job as a teenage ranch-hand and well, that's saying something now, isn't it?!); this work ethic served me when I went back to school later on. Let's see, what else? Oh yeh, it was pretty nice that I had somewhere to go at age twenty-nine other than the homeless shelter when I was bah-roke. I don't think I knew before that time, how much my parents did in fact love me, that they would welcome me home in spite of my mistakes without shaming me to my face or to others. This was an important fact that I had to throw into the end sum of it all.

Last but not least, Fancy Francie had cared enough about me to tell me the truth: she turned out to be, one of a very few people whose words of caution about the Lug I was able to actually absorb. Everyone said it, yet I could only *hear* the truth from, as it turns out, three people: a therapist, a pastor and Fancy Francie. Even though it took me five more years to effectively apply her advice and break up with the Lug for good, the memory of her opinion factored in, even though I didn't see her much after that. Assessing it now, her words were worth the physical debt incurred, even if that had been the only redeemable attribute.

However, the content of this grand epiphany did not steep into my frontal lobe for many years after. The experience of G. Louise was an absolute grown-up, grad school-like education. I gave a lot to it, and it in turn, gave a lot back to me. Therefore, in terms of profits and loss, it probably left me in the black. But all I knew then was the red nature of my bank account along with my self-image, that I was now twenty-nine and still did not have a dime to my name. The day I sold G. Louise and signed the paperwork, I went straight from the lawyers' office "home" to finish packing up the condo to make the humble drive of shame over to my folks' place. At twenty-nine, I felt unaccomplished and unsuccessful. I laid on a twin bed in my parent's guest room on a red, white and blue-checked pouffy comforter, next to the other twin bed that would be Jeannine's ('cause she was broke too).

A nice man from church named Harry Summers (see again with the names? That really is his name), felt sorry for me and gave me a job in his insurance office, which, can I just tell you? Going from the glam of the fashion world and the hip nature of recording studios, to selling insurance? Wow—now that my Friends, is a stretch. I'll never forget learning how to read the forms I had to eventually lead customers through and I asked Harry, "What does this word stand for, right here with this little box next to it? It says 'ind.'" I was pointing at it with my pencil. "Does that stand for 'Individual?'"

"Oh" he said. That abbreviation stands for 'Indigent.'" [Sidebar: in hindsight, I suspect Harry Summers must've thought my guess on the abbreviation sounded like a pageant-girl answer?!]

"Hmmmm," I thought, "...Indigent." I'm not even sure I know what that means, but I'm pretty sure I am indigent. I am Individually Indigent.

Hence, what did I have to lose by trying out selling Amway along with my glitzy new insurance job? Geesh Louise!

Fifteen: What Are You Doing Here?

Remember the Drunk Church Boy? Well, it wasn't long after the Scotch-cheeseburger-church-birthday party incident that I began to think Burk wasn't the one for me. Let's face it: after years of mistreatment from the Lug, my capacity for screw-ups was nonexistent. And it was a prophetic move to end the relationship because just a few days before that church service, we had been at my Mom's for Thanksgiving. My older sister and brother-in-law were in from Colorado and after a long Thanksgiving Day celebration, he said farewell to Burk with this lovely parting salutation: "Hey Burk, it was nice to meet you. Too bad you won't be around next year...." and his voice trailed off as if he couldn't believe he'd actually said it out loud. Lane is perhaps the most non-controversial person I've ever met. He would never place himself in the middle of conflict (unlike my sister) so I know it must have been that I truly had paraded so many eligible bachelors by my family that he really just couldn't help himself.

Burk nervously laughed it off, but little did either of us know his fate had already been sealed. Three days after Thanksgiving, he came to church smelling like a scotch distillery and it was about a week or so after, that I began inching myself away from him until a week before Christmas when I'd declared it over. Burk, an attorney, tried to argue me out of my decision, treating me in the conversation first, like a client, and then as opposing council. He did not treat me like a hostile witness though, because I think he could tell my mind was made up.

Then a few days after Christmas, he'd called explaining that he'd gotten me a gift and wondered if he could drop it off [what is it with Christmas and non-boyfriends giving gifts?!]. Feeling guilty and terrible about how quickly I'd cut him out of my life (as quickly as I'd embraced dating him), I caved. He stopped by on a Sunday afternoon. Now please understand: I had been sneaking around with the Lug again and it was Christmas time. People exchange gifts at Christmas time. I say "sneaking" because even my family didn't know I was giving the Lug his twenty-fourth chance to become a man who would honor me. So, the Lug did what he always did and swooped me up with expensive dinners and lavish gifts. Burk's call was a last minute thing and what happened next was ironic because it mirrors a scene from a film based on my favorite Jane Austen novel.

In Austen's novel, *Sense and Sensibility*, the protagonist Marianne, although in love with the seemingly dashing Willoughby, is also adored from afar by the stoic Colonel Brandon. In Emma Thompson's film adaptation, there's a scene where Brandon brings flowers to Marianne. Brandon arrives right before Willoughby, who brings her a bouquet as well, which Marianne considers to be the more intriguing of the two. A well-intended gift was out-shown by a manipulative *gift-giver*, and it was clear the protagonist made the common mistake of believing what she wanted to see, instead of what was actually there: a gentleman bringing her something heartfelt and lovely, versus a scoundrel who brought her some handpicked-weeds. She thought she preferred the scoundrel and the weeds.

And so it played out in my real life: Colonel Brandon [Burk] stopped over with a gift for me. As I opened the front door and Burk walked in, he noticed over my shoulder and on the table, a munificent gift from the Lug: an orange vase the size of the Rock of Gibraltar, with birds of paradise, anthuriums, and other accoutrements reaching towards the ceiling. It said, "Hi, I'm bigger and much more impressive than your offering." Burk, feeling intimidated and bearing the shrunken nature of a defeated soldier, lifted his gift over to me like an orphan boy in Dickens', *Oliver*. He refrained from saying "Please Surrrr, may I have sum-mor" along with the gift, but for goodness sake he might as well have! To say I felt bad standing there in front of the Lug's enormous orange vase, the symbol representing Burk's exit from my life, while Burk himself handed over a wooden black box, was almost more than I could take!

When I opened it, I felt even worse because it was a collection of silver wine bottle toppers fitted into velvet sections of the box, each one having their own perfectly fitted nest. It was clearly something he put time and thought into and I almost refused to accept it because I felt so bad! What a juxtaposition, huh? The Lug calls the florist and sends the most expensive arrangement in a vase from a local art gallery I'd been eyeing and overtly telling him I'd wanted for years. Meanwhile, Burk had spent only eight weeks paying attention to my likes and dislikes and gave me something heartfelt, thoughtful and appropriate. And...I'm sending Burk home?

But upon his departure, I exhaled and thought to myself, "Well thank goodness THAT'S over." Break-ups suck but this one left a mark and I was grateful to not have the pressure of anticipating anymore exchanges with Burk. Hasta la vista, Baby! I never have to see you again.

So....imagine my surprise at seeing Burk just two weeks later....at *my* church. What are you doing here? I have a life, it doesn't include you, and I told myself (and others) I was being "stalked." Which... looking back, is mind-numbingly arrogant! It's a free country and he can worship God wherever he wants to (although in fairness to me, I was convinced he didn't actually know God very well, which I'd figured was a chicken scratch in my column for the stalking argument.) At some point after the second time I saw him at church, I decided that my attitude needed to change though and I did manage to change it, but I also avoided him.

But that Stinker actually stayed around! He hung out in the "Singles" group which I avoided like the plague. I didn't want to associate myself with the other singles because you know...it might rub off on my reputation even more, that I was...gasp...actually *single!* (I guess I thought there were degrees of singleness... as in, one could be less single by not associating themselves with other singles.) This, now I see, had also been the height of stupid. No actually, it was asinine. As if people didn't already know I was unmarried and thirty-two? Paahlease.

Burk not only hung out with the singles group though, he became close friends with the couple that led the singles group. He started making friends in the church outside of the singles group and if that weren't enough, he started dating another girl FROM the singles group named Sheila. Right in front of my face—yes he did.

I pretended that it didn't bother me. I thought about this on occasion when I was home, tapping my fingers on the window sill I was sitting next to, or on the edge of my laptop keyboard while I was sitting cross-legged on the coach. How dare he be over me already? I counted the months up on my fingers: one, two three, four...five... SIX?! Wow, *six* months had passed since we'd broken up. If he wanted to date a singles-group girl, I guess I couldn't argue. And it also bugged me because Cole had gone out with the same girl for awhile before he married Jeannine (because as I said before, datable people were slim pickins in this neck of the woods). It was all too weird.

No matter. Burk has his own life. Whatever. Whut. Evv. Fer.

It was a shame that it hadn't worked out between Burk and me. I mean, we had the best story of anyone meeting anyone ever. I had been out with a friend of mine named Lizzy, who had called me the day before, begging me to go with to a bachelorette party. "Please Robbi? I don't want to go at all and if you come, I'll actually know someone besides the bride." So thinking again of Penny's advice about going places and not sitting home, drowning in loneliness, I begrudgingly attended a bachelorette party of someone I hardly knew. After a rousing game of pin-the-penis-on-the testicles, we were each handed a cucumber and a sharp knife and asked to carve it like the shape of the penis of our significant other. I did not have a significant other at this precise moment, but even if I did, I wouldn't have done it because you know...I had some class left. Lizzy gave me this look as if to say, "Seriously? There is NO way I'm cutting this in the shape of Joe's winky or otherwise I'll be DEAD." I nodded back to her look.

Shockingly, the other attendees must have been drunk already because they did it, gripping their representations upwards and sideways with quizzical expressions, studying their specimens to make certain they were carved exactly right. This was a group of 30-year-old women, mind you. All completely fine with it. One said, "I think Tom's is more round at the tip" as she focused on whether or not she would try to re-carve it in order to do justice to Tom's tip. Another said, "Gosh...Donny's shaft is thinner than this cuke I carved. It's about this width." She held her hand in the shape of Donny's width. And so on and so on and so on. That was it. Lizzy and I quietly disappeared to the kitchen to eat Chex mix and discreetly toss our cukes in the garbage.

Eventually, the party was being moved to the Kirby Grill in Grand Haven, where the bride wore a t-shirt that said "suck for a buck," with lifesavers sown directly onto it. Lizzy and I were proud to find ourselves prudes. Neither of us thought going around flirting with others was a particularly good idea once engaged, especially the weekend before you were to marry your betrothed. So once we got to the Kirby, we disappeared to a couple of barstools on the other side of the restaurant/bar. Sitting on my right was a redhead called, "Rusty," whom I would later find out was also known as Burk. He was with a buddy and wow, this buddy? He could sell ice cubes to the North Pole. His name was Decker and he was a fast talker, a big smiler and well, slightly inappropriate because he paid a dollar to bite a Lifesaver off the bride's t-shirt. Before he hopped off his barstool to go flirt with the bride, he said, "Hey—this is my buddy, 'Rusty!'" Burk looked and smiled a "because I have to" smile. Decker said, "Hey Blondie, by the way, what's your name?"

"Robyn."

"Huh. Are you from around here???"

"Yeh, actually I live a few blocks away over on Lake Street."

And Decker, with his jaw dropping slightly, his brows up high and his eyes bugging out a little, sounded as surprised as he looked, exclaiming, "Well, whadda ya know?! I thought I knew every single girl in this town!" And it was as arrogant as it sounded. Lizzy's eyes were darting back and forth between me and him, and I guess it's important to mention here that Lizzy's husband was the Lug's best friend and business partner, but she'd always been on my side of the Lug feuds. She knew the Lug and I were on the outs and she was looking from smooth-talking Decker and then back to me, looking between the two of us a couple of times like watching a tennis match almost, as if to say, "Don't do it Robbi. He's a player!" A. Noth. Er. Player!" Meanwhile, Burk just stared into his beer trying to remain as anonymous as he could. He seemed as uncomfortable with his bud's behavior as Lizzy and I had been with the penis games.

What Lizzy didn't know was that I wasn't really interested in Decker or Rusty/Burk for that matter either. I just wanted to get the hell out. Yet, I couldn't help responding to Deck's shock and dismay that there existed a local single gal in this town he had miraculously never met, if even for the mere entertainment value alone. So I said, "Yeh Decker, I don't really go to 'the bar' much. 'Not a barfly," and I wasn't because nothing good ever comes from getting wasted in bars among strangers. I'd learned that when I was in my early twenties. So now if I went out to "the bar," it was with a date but not by myself or even with "the girls."

My retort seemed to bore Decker so with that, he headed over to "suck for a buck," which left me, Lizzy and Burk sitting there. So just being friendly, I said to Rusty, "What do you do, Rusty?"

Rusty looked up from his beer and said,

"I'm an attorney." Wow Rusty—you respond just like Carlose—no further explaining or elaborating. As with Carlose, I tried again.

"Do you work here in town?"

"Nope."

Okay, that's it. I'm outtta here! I looked at Lizzy and asked her if she was ready to go too, and she responded, "I thought you'd NEVER ask!" I hopped off the barstool, grabbed my bag and headed for the door. Lizzy was on my heels. As soon as I went through the turnstile and made it to the street, Burk magically appeared. I never saw him get up and follow. So there we stood, Lizzy, Burk and I hanging out on the sidewalk. "Where you goin' so fast?" Burk asked, and that was the first time I'd seen a genuine look on his face. His eyes were the color of blueberry Kool-Aid.

"I have to go—I'm singing in church tomorrow and it's getting late. 'Not good for the chords [pointing to my throat] to be in loud smoky places, so I'm retiring for the night."

"You sing??" and before I could respond, Lizzy, almost shouting, excitedly piped in with, "Yeh, and she's AWESOME!" She was egging him on! Okay, now I'm blushing. *Really Chica?*

"Well, what are you singing tomorrow?" he asked, actually looking interested.

"Amazing Grace—it's this four part harmony acapella thing..."

He goes, "Well, I used to sing a little and I know that song!" He was grinning now...continuously. "Sing some for me right now."

"No." *Okay maybe I'll consider it, if it will make you go away...* I continued. "No, that's okay...I really couldn't..." and see...here is the reason why I really didn't want to: when I was a kid, my parents, beaming with pride in their talented daughter, would bring me down from the upstairs where children were usually kept in order to remain unseen and unheard. Yet, they would make this one exception during their dinner parties for me to sing for their party guests, which was... EVERY weekend. So now that I'm grown up and all, I understand this was a compliment but back then, I was embarrassed and truthfully until this day, I would rather sing for 10,000 nameless faces in an arena than for four people in my own living room. I didn't like being my parents' dog and pony show. In their defense they were both musicians, my Dad a professional horn player and my Mom a vocalist, and they both had perfect pitch, which they passed to me. So I'm pretty sure they wouldn't have paraded me past their company-du-jour had I sucked. Furthermore, they were teetotalers: what else were they to do for entertainment when the dinner portion of their evening was over? (But I imagined crickets—lots of crickets.) However, their lack-of-booze defense aside, I still didn't like it. Hence, it is the reason I resisted Burk's sidewalk request.

But he wasn't taking "no" for an answer. The more I sheepishly tried not to, the more Lizzy encouraged him to make me. And then, the more he was happy to oblige her. Intense blushing continued to light up my cheeks and I was glad it was dark outside. I sputtered out, "no, really you guys, that's okay..." while I shrugged my shoulders and smiled in a self-conscious manner. Burk must have thought, "There's more than one way to skin a cat," because he decided to start singing for me.

"Come 'on," he said, elbowing in my direction, "Amazing gra.... that's how it goes right?" He started again: "Amazing Grace how sweet the sound...."

I was dying.

He continued: "...That saved a wretch..." —At least his singing was in tune...

Okay, now I felt like I had to join him because he was singing by himself, naked in front of the Kirby Grill by...himself (Settle down: "naked" is a term musicians use for a vocal when it's acapella or supported by only acoustic accompaniment. He wasn't literally naked. His vocal was naked.) Musicians worry for nakedly exposed comrades and seek to fill in, so the other musician will feel "supported." And even when the song calls for it and has to be done that way, like a flute solo in the middle of an orchestral arrangement with 100 other symphony musicians sitting around the flautist, everyone has to fight the urge to join in and prays the soloist gets through it without a mistake...'cause it's hard.

So instinct kicked in and I joined him. He sang the whole chorus and I filled in here and there, albeit SHEEPISHLY. This was not a resounding rendition or something I wanted a passerby to notice, but I figured this way, he would stop sooner and he was in fact satisfied to finish that one section, without going on. That's how I could tell he wasn't wasted, but was friendly for real.

Lizzy didn't help matters because she applauded. Again—I was dying. "All right, Guys.." (referring to them as a group because they seemed to be in one, since they were rooting for the same outcome with the song), "I gotta go. Good night!" I smiled and hollered over my shoulder as I headed to my car with a wave.

I wasn't sure if Burk went back into the Kirby or left or what, but I saw Lizzy waving back towards me and heading toward her own car. That was that.

Three days later however, there was a knock at my door. I lived in an attic apartment at the time, that had a separate entrance in the back of an old glorious house with a wrap around porch on Lake Street in Grand Haven. The apartment had no laundry, garbage disposal or even a shower. It had a bathtub only, with a hand held sprayer for hair-washing in the bathtub. It was a teeny weeny space, but it was quaint and cool and most-importantly, it was mine. But given the geometrics of the location, no one would have ever known there was a separate residence up there. It was private. So, whenever there was knock on the door, it was either the landlord (who rarely stopped by), or it was a friend I had invited over. There were no random knockers. Even the UPS guy left stuff on the porch down below. So anywho, I had just gotten out of the bath and had on this humongous fuzzy robe with a pink poodle on the back and a pink dog bone on the front, with a towel wrapped on top of my head and there it was—a surprise knock on the door. Assuming it was the landlord, I cracked the door open. Before I could ascertain who it even was, the person almost yelling, shouted, "I'm not a stalker!" Before I could say anything, he continued in a defensive manner, "I met you the other night at Kirby. I'm Deck, Rusty's friend." It was all coming back to me. This was the guy who sucked for a buck and flirted with the bride. He looked different when he wasn't in a drunken haze.

"Ummm....what are you doing here?" I asked as I was still peeking out though two inches of a slightly ajar door with a robe up to my chin and a towel on my head. I'm not even sure my eyebrows were showing. But anyway, it was a fair question. Decker sounded apologetic, like he knew it was weird,

"Well...ahh... ya know my friend Rusty from the other night? He really liked you. I live here on the Lakeshore and my friend lives in Grand Rapids. I told him I would see if I could find you for him. He would like to ask you out."

I quizzically raised two towel-covered eyebrows [because I never learned how to raise just one and can't until this day—but if there were ever to be a one-eyebrow raising moment, this would have been it.]

"How... ha..howw...umm... how did you find me exactly?"

"Well, remember the other night when I met you at the Kirby? You said you lived, 'over there on Lake Street?' Rusty woke up the next day and said, 'I've gotta find that blonde.' So, since I run everyday, I decided to run up and down this street and I thought to myself, 'If I were a blondie named 'Robyn,' which house would I live in?'" The towel on my head was getting heavy now from my two raised eyebrows, which were so high by this point, I think they were causing wrinkles. He continued, "So....then today I saw your landlord out front raking leaves and I stopped and asked him if he knew a girl named 'Robyn' that lived around here and he told me to go around back, that you lived here. He....said it was okay...".

I didn't know whether to be scared to death by my landlord's lack of security or impressed with Decker's tenacity. I think I was both. Keep in mind, I was still peeking at him through two inches of a cracked door in a pink and white-poodled terrycloth bathrobe looking like the babe I'm sure both he and ol' "Rusty" remembered they'd met....

"Hmmm. Okay." I was was pushing my lips together and moving them from left to right and back again because I was thinking.... Yes, I was thinking and thinking. Then I said, "Hmmm" again and finally decided it was okay. "Look Deck—it is Decker isn't it? So, here's the deal. I'm in an on-again-off-again very complicated...frankly dysfunctional....relationship and well...I'm trying to figure it out. Based on *that*, if your friend..uh...'Rusty' is it?" Decker nodded. "...Then tell Rusty if wants to call me, he's welcome to...stay there a second, I'll go get my card." I shut the door and thought that even if I weren't somewhere between here and nowhere with the Lug, and even if "Rusteeee" were a nice guy, he'd probably never call me anyway after his best friend saw me me like this. I looked down and took an assessment: Wow—I am one hot chick. Cah-lass-ee!

I went back to the door and slipped my card through the two-inch crack, thinking nothing would come from it. I smiled and Decker left. And in case you're concerned, I realize this little speech I gave to Decker was similar to the one I've previously mentioned that I'd also given Stephano at first, regarding the dysfunction and...fluidity of my availability. (I like that word as descriptive for my situation: "fluid." I mean, "eff'ed up" is closer to the truth but for now I was going with "fluid.")

After Decker left, I stood thinking. Hmmmmm. I thought. Ever since taking Penny's advice to go out with anyone and everyone who asks, I did a lot of hmmmmmm-ing. There were a great deal many moments to hmmmmmmm about.

But anyway, you do see, right, that Burk and I did have the best story of anyone meeting anyone anywhere?! How many people end up dating because his friend went looking for a girl, without a phone number or address and ends up finding her without Facebook, LinkedIn, email, phone records, or the internet. It was 1997. He hadn't even hired a private investigator. I mean, some people already had PCs and email but I didn't! So what—Decker and Rusty had email? An internet search, without any information but a girl's first name didn't turn up much back then, especially if her phone was unlisted.

Decker was not intimidated. He'd put his positive salesman's attitude to work for him and said, "No problem, Bud—this town isn't that big and like I said, I know where NOT to look because I know every other single girl soooooo, I will find her for you." He had a street name, and a first name and it only took him three days, in spite of the fact that he worked full time. That's a pretty good friend, right?! [And although he did have to sacrifice some of his time, that he'd normally spend flirting with all of the single girls in town, he did, in fact, already know in order to find me, I think this made me appreciate it even more.]

So now, as I tapped my fingers on the window sill, sitting cross-legged on my couch, while thinking about Burk dating Sheila from church, I figured it stunk that Burk and I hadn't worked out just given the way we met. I mean, it was a complete waste: he had met Sheila at the "singles group." Oh that's a sexy story to tell your future grandchildren! Wow—I'll bet they'll be impressed! Just imagine little 10-year-old granddaughters beaming with joy: "Oh please Grandad, tell it to us again how you met Grammy???!!"

Grandpa Burk: clearing his throat, "Well...Uggghhh....I went to church one day and went to this er...uh...this singles group, ya see? And ...uhhh...it was there that I first saw your skinny little no-breasted, flat-butted Grammy and we lived happily ever after. Ahem." Okay, I know that's mean, but every girl does that when they're jealous right? Picks apart the other woman? I mean gheesopete, what had poor Sheila ever done to me? Nothing. She was really nice in fact, and actually pretty funny. One time she drove around with plastic tulips hanging out the door of her car on purpose to protest the Holland Tulip Time Festival (because it crowds 200,000 additional people into a town they can't all fit into). She made her car look like she'd driven through the tulip fields and run them over. It was funny She *was* amusing. I *did* see what he saw in her. Damn it.

But what right did I think I had, especially since I had broken up with Burk to go back to the Lug, and so now I, in another Lug-off-period, could not look at Burk as an option, just because he stayed around and found God and Sheila at my church. Still, Burk and Sheila met at a singles' group, whereas I had met Burk in a glorious romantic setting! (I began to romanticize the past, as the singing-sidewalk incident now seemed to be a rather lovely moment instead of the uncomfortable way it made me writhe around inside my skin at the time. I was reasoning out how cute it was that Burk stood there with abandonment and didn't care what anybody thought, including me, and just sang Amazing Grace. That's romantic, right?)

I squeezed it out of my mind though and besides, he was taken. And, I'd already told Cate along with everybody else, including Lizzy, that I wasn't attracted to him. And I wasn't. I didn't like redheads. It didn't matter either, that meeting Burk was a great story which even encompassed a good book title: *Bathrobes, Sidewalk Solos and a Guy Named Rusty*...One has to admit, it did have a certain ring to it. But no matter. For the last time, I don't like redheads, or rust for that matter.

Sixteen:
The Rolling Stones vs. Robyn Brodie
Ya Can't Always Get What you Want vs Ya Always Want What Ya Can't Have

It wasn't only bugging me that Burk was taken, I was infinitely bugged that the Lug was also taken. He was dating a girl named Tamryn. He seemed into Tamryn, or so I'd *heard* from Lizzy on occasion. Usually I didn't want her to tell me anything because I was trying SO hard not to get hooked back on him, because of course, I knew it was a codependent relationship and the more we went around and round, the more we'd just go round and round. The Walking-Dead-Gerbil-Wheel was not one I really wanted, but when we were apart I had a tendency to romanticize and maximize the good between us while minimizing the bad; in reality there was so so so so so much very very very bad.

On paper, the Lug looked like a catch, but he was troubled inside. He was too introspective. He was like Anikin Skywalker, always fighting between the right side and the evil side of the force. When he wanted me back, he showed me he was a Jedi Knight. When we got back together, his Jedi ways were fleeting and he wore that evil sullen look as if something powerful had control over him. It sounds dramatic. In fact, just telling you this makes me want to make a gagging sound with my throat. Ay. yi. yi. There isn't another universal way to explain why, (as I beat this metaphor-allusion combo to death), that as Padmé I loved him anyway, yet knew it wasn't right for me. Okay relax—I'm not comparing myself to Natalie Portman for goodness sake—only to the character of Padmé in the sense that love pushed aside her good judgment in staying committed to an up-and-down-back-forth man. No, I don't think I'm royalty like Padmé or a political diplomat either! 'Just a girl who loved a complicated mess and was more than addicted to the need of it turning out successfully.

The Lug and Tamryn were hot and heavy; "Serious" actually, was the word being tossed around. So you know how we always want what we can't have? I began pining for The Lug. Yes, *this* after Burk and after Skip and after Nate. Please hear the theme from the movie, "Love Story," or theme music from any soap opera that was popular during the 1990's. 'Gotchyor music in place? Okay, so here it is: I started writing to the Lug in a journal every night with messages I would share with him if we were to ever get back together, as if it were some type of present telepathic communication.

Slight pause to focus on a bed of violins playing a pass of la-la-la-la-lah from *Love Story*.

I wrote down the sentiments of what I loved about him *la la la la lah*—there were acknowledgments of where I thought I'd personally made mistakes ('cause I wasn't so forthcoming about those on prior occasions) *la la la la la la la la la la lah lah*. I also wrote about all of the dreams I had for our future. It was a nightly ritual as I longed for another chance *la la la la lah*.

One morning during this cheesy phase of Lug pine-journaling, the phone rang and and it was Burk. He said, "Rob—what are you doing today? Would you meet me for coffee for a half hour? I really need to talk with you about something..."

"Hmm," I thought, speaking of hot and heavy, he is dating Sheila now so this seems odd...

"Surrrre...," I answered, although hesitant and then asked, "Can you give me an idea what about??"

"I'd rather just talk about it when I see you. I'll drive up to Grand Haven—see you at the Coffee Grounds in about an hour?"

"Sure, okay." It was Saturday and the Coffee Grounds was a ten minute walk from my house. So I met him there (but not before I changed my clothes, put on some make up, touched up my hair—even though I wasn't interested in him. Whuuhht? A girl does these things...) But anyway, I saw him smiling at me when I arrived and we sat at a little square table on the sidewalk under a coiffed crabapple tree. He looked cute with his beachy shorts and his shirt tucked in the front only. He was tan too and had a few freckles on the bridge of his nose. "Hey there. What's goin' on?" Then he took his sun glasses off, leaned across the table, looked right in my eyes and said,

"I need to know something, Rob. Sheila and I are at a place where we need to take our relationship to the next level. Before I can do that, I need to know....if I could ever...could ever...have another chance with you..." I started to answer him and he interrupted me, continuing with his hand up, "You DON"T have to make a decision right now and I'm not asking you to commit to marriage or anything like that!! I'm just asking if there's a chance for us to date again." And he stopped talking and just looked at me. UUUgggghhhh! I so liked this guy. I couldn't believe I still mattered to him, and also, I was caught off guard because of his overt courage to say so, which left me feeling flattered and somewhat surprised; the push-pull of the different emotions confused me for a sec. What does one say?? So I gave him a smile that kind of looked like an apology and offered,

"Ya know...I've been hoping and praying for another chance with 'the Lug.'" (I didn't actually refer to him as "the Lug"—I said his real name. To be honest, I hadn't thought up the nickname yet, even though I knew he was a burden and that the relationship was a weighted cause. I also lugged around the darkness he was shrouded in, the failures in our relationship and the desperation that it had to amount to *something* after the wasteful investment.) But to Burk, I used his name.

I shook my head sideways, as if to say "I know...I know, it's stupid— it's crazy...." I didn't have to say it out loud to know that's what my head shaking meant. Burk knew too. He said, "Okay—well I needed to ask and I'm thankful I did. Then he stood up to leave and I went to give him a half hug, like an arm squeeze around the shoulder. But we walked into each other in an awkward way; we were pulling up the chairs and getting steady on our feet and it just happened. We hugged. Really tight. Burk said later he walked away from that moment thinking, "*Okay—she said no but her body just told me yes. I'm so utterly confused...*"

But he took my word for it and three months later, I'd heard that he was going home to meet Shelia's family for Thanksgiving in Chicago. They are going to get engaged soon. I assumed it. But anyway, back to the Lug and me...

So I continued to write in my journal and Lizzy, who wasn't supposed to tell me anything, was...willing to tell me stuff whenever I was overcome with morbid curiosity and stooped to ask her. She said that the Lug and his new girlfriend seemed serious, but in private moments he'd confided in Joe (or so he thought they were private) that he wasn't sure about her. That was my "in."

I broke down. I called him! I said I wanted to get together and talk. He agreed, reluctantly. I went over to his place and poured out my heart. "I still love you." I still feel like we are one person. Here, I've written down my thoughts about it. Will you just read this??" I was stammering. He was reluctant. He was of course brooding as usual, like Anakin Skywalker.

"Tamryn would flip out if she knew you were here Robyn. I don't know. I miss you too, but I'm invested with her now...."

"Just think about it," and before he could respond, I left and peeled out of his driveway. I took my journal though because I didn't sense it was the right time to leave it with him.

An excruciating week later, at the end of September, he called me to explain that he had told Tamryn he needed time and "space" to think things over. He asked if I would come over. That night, I resurfaced on his doorstep expecting a teary reunion between us as was our "usual," yet he was cold. After a semi-polite greeting, I was there for thirty minutes before he said anything to me. I pushed the issue because I didn't know what to think. Shaking and desperate, I half-asked, half-shouted, "So are we back together or not? What is this? What does it mean?"

He snapped at me: "Why do you ALWAYS need a definition??!! Why can't you just go with it?"

"Uh, Lug—it's been seven years. I'm here forever or I am NOT here at all Dude. Pick." I was staring at him, still shaking as I set my journal down on the nearest surface, a little table by the front door.

He softened, "I pick yes." In spite of an enormous sigh of relief, I still suspected it wasn't real, but I was trying to convince my inner core that hoping for real and knowing it was real were the same. The inner core argued, because it wasn't more than an hour later that I felt compelled to test it: I began talking about the future, asking about events such as, "where and when do you want to get married," and "when should we tell our families?" I was clearly pushing him because he'd made all of these promises before. Oh, not to mention I was ahem... thirty-three years old now and he had just turned forty. Then he yelled, "I won't tell you TODAY! Stop asking me!"

That was it: I ripped off the Tiffany bracelet he'd given to me a year or so earlier on another one of our cat-and-mouse reunions, (that I'd later rightly suspected had also been a bribe), and I threw it at him. It nicked his elbow and landed on the counter behind him. I grabbed my purse and abruptly left.

Talk about some wrecked hope? As an aside, can I just ask: why do people say they want something when they don't want something? Why do people tell you they are in the same place and agree with you and then they clearly do not agree with you? If he had said he didn't want to get married this time, I wouldn't have gone over there. The part I confess responsibility for though, is believing he could possibly say and mean it. I didn't know who I felt worse about: his actions or my own stupid self denial.

I spent two angry days weeping and recoiled in my house. I unplugged the phone. I didn't want him to be able to get to me. I plugged it back in on occasion to call my Mom or Jeannine, so they wouldn't suspect I'd tried it with him again and/or so they wouldn't worry about me if they couldn't reach me, but then I would immediately unplug it again. Nearing the end of the second day, in spite of my efforts to avoid any contact with the Lug, a box showed up on my doorstep—from a distance I could see that it must have been "dropped off" instead of professionally delivered, because the top of the box was folded over like a college student's hasty packing job when they move home for the summer. As I got closer, I could also see there was no written address or postage on it so I ran at it and tore it open! It was haphazardly stuffed full of every picture, ticket stub and memory the Lug and I had ever shared. It was double the size of a shoe box. I was so angry, I stomped with it in-tow over to the garbage can, opened the lid and dropped it in. All of it. JUST like that. It was garbage day tomorrow so I wheeled the can to the street with dignified intent.

The day after garbage day, a package arrived in the mail. I immediately recognized the Lug's scrawl. It was a padded envelope, like it held something valuable inside. I tore it open and it was....?

My journal! My journal?? Oh...that's right...I must've left it when I stormed out last time. He's returning it to me now I guess, since he forgot it when he dumped all of our memories in a box on the doorstep the other day. Then I lifted the leather cover and began glancing through its pages, and began to notice some red ink marks. I turned page after page breathing deep, almost hyperventilating as I took in his angry scrawl on almost every golden-edged page. He had defaced my sentiments and longings. Certain words were circled with a red pen next to them that read, "You don't really believe that!" Or, there was an arrow in the margin pointing to a section that he'd scratched, "You're a LIAR!" and "I wish I'd never met you" and "I hate you Robyn!" Remember how I told you about the stark contrast between my break-up with Stephano and my final break from the Lug because with Steph there was so much love and the Lug was embroiled in deep yuck and how it was a different kind of sad? Now you have a shred of that yuck.

I don't think I've ever felt more alone in my life than on that day. I'd pushed all of the supportive loving people out of my confidence and inner circle. I couldn't call Jeannine or my Mom or any of my friends. There is no one who would have approved that I even tried to reconcile with him again! I mean, if I'd started a conversation with ...Jeannine say for example, that went, "You're not gonna believe it: the Lug defaced my journal...and he— "

"Since WHEN were you even considering going back to him???!!!" She would be shrieking it at me or flipping out in such a manner and I would have deserved it. I'm not picking on Jeannine—she'd react just like any one person out of a group of fifteen people I'd previously confided in would have now responded. My point is that there was nowhere to turn with my discomfort and self-loathing this time. So, I turned inward and about two weeks later, I called Stephano for the first time and told him I would go out with him after all. That's how Stephano started and that's why when it ended, I was broken-hearted. After what it took to peel the Lug's control off from me, like a tightened fist of gnarled fingers that had to be pried off one by one, and then, to make it stay off of me for good, it took believing there was someone else. I had just dabbled around with Nate and Skip and Burk really...But Stephano made me *believe* it in my soul.

Seventeen:
Ode to Styx: I Got Toohoo Much...Time on My Hayands

In my angst in getting over Stephano and in those dark days that followed, I needed to fill up all of the extra hours of my time that I had given to our relationship—and boy, did I ever have empty hours of time, even though I was a full time student with three part time jobs [which included managing a family-business office, singing the anthem at the Griffins and working at a boutique in town. In addition, I also put in a great deal of time to help and take care of my Dad.] Other than these commitments, every single minute of my time had been spent with Stephano. In fact, he downright ran me ragged: other than the Buffett concerts, Italian family reunions (re-un-ionnzz, as in plural reunions—there were many) and Stephano's "professional" softballs games that I was expected to attend 'doncha know... [...in spite of hindsight sarcasm, I actually did attend all of his softball games since it was just expected.] Also, Stephano had a truckload of friends. The summer we dated, we went to six weddings, only one of which was a friend of mine. But anyway, Stephano's social butterfly status had dragged me along to many an event. But now? It. Was. Quiet.

Filling my lonely hours meant opportunities such as hangin' out with my Dad even more, which always presented an interesting list of ways for me to be helpful and feel companionship. The list includes but was not limited to:

-Pediatrist appointments where his Hobbit-like toe nails were professionally trimmed.

-Occupational therapy appointments that he attended in a begrudging fashion, even though they never did any good at achieving his long term memory. He'd come out of there trying to remember my first name when I picked him up. It didn't matter to me though because even if he couldn't say it right, I knew that he knew it was me.

-Frequent lunches out, which he always paid for so it was a deal for me. Unfortunately they were always at the Bil-Mar, a restaurant which had a fantastic beach-view location, but had an unfortunate prehistoric menu. It'd been boasting the same steak and baked potato menu for fifty years. Still, it's where he wanted to go three times per week, so we went three times per week. Every time this server-dude would set down my Dad's steak order that was burned to the consistency of shoe leather ['cause that's how a guy who came of age during the Great Depression ordered and still orders his meat...], my father would say a hearty, "Oh BOY!" Dad "oh Boy'ed" me and the server-dude three times per week.

So, my Dad helped fill some hours, which was also a big help to my Mom. It was win/win. It was less lonely for my Dad and me, and she had more time.

I was sick of dating though. Sick, Sick, SICK of it! I thought I would never go on another date again. I was not interested. And there's no one who'd disagree that I hadn't put in sufficient time. Oh, I'd taken Penny's advice for sure! It hadn't worked. And since I am a perfectionist over-achiever who brought my best to every project, I had given this cause more than my all....which is perhaps why I felt like I would now hold up my middle finger to the prospect of "Husband Finding." Goodbye!

There was one desperate moment in the middle of this conclusive-assumptive period, after a long, long, looooohhhhng lonely Saturday where I had weak moment. I called up Cole and asked him, ...as if I'd never asked him this question before, keeping as much light in my voice as I could, I asked, "Hey...do you have any friends who are still single?" Awkward silence. Stammering on, I squeaked out, "I mean, ya know, ya can't blame a girl for askin', right?" I tried to get the shoulder-shrugging stance I was taking on this question, to come through in my voice into the phone. Cole cleared his throat and said,

"Ah....No Rob; Ya kind flew through 'em all." And that was that. He was right. I had. Let's see: I'd gone out with Brad Bouvier, Cole's one-time college buddy turned Chicago real estate mogul, but it was just too weird—like going on a date with a cousin. We'd gone to a mutual friend's wedding together but Jeannine and Cole were there too, so it didn't feel different than like a Sunday dinner at my Mom's. Then I dated Trent for a season, a guy Cole knew way back from high school, but he was freshly separated and on his way to being a divorced, single dad and yep—that's right! Cole didn't like it and was therefore righteously indignant about the fact that Trent was still "technically married" even through the cops had come to break up a domestic dispute when Trent's ex threw a lamp through the front plate-glass window with their baby in the room, so I was pretty sure he wouldn't be reconciling. Still, Cole wouldn't let it go: "He's married, Robyn! You are not this desperate!"

"He likes me! You haven't seen him since high school graduation and *just* started hanging out with him again—I just met him for the first time a couple of weeks ago! I'm not the reason he's getting divorced for goodness sake! His ex is a freakshow, with or without me in the picture."

"Get out of the picture. Please stop dating him anyway?! It's...it's... just GROSS!"

At the time, I'd thought Cole was being a prude. But as usual, he turned out to be right about that one too, arguing that I would just be the "transition girl," and of course I was, and so of course it was short-lived. Oh yeh, you've already heard about Bobby. I finally capitulated to one date with him, but he had to take me home right at the beginning of the date, a few minutes after we took our first sip of margarita at Chi Chi's, because it didn't mix with some new medicine I had just been prescribed and I started falling asleep at the table. This one goes down in my book as simple par for the course. Was I embarrassed the next day? Not really. Which just demonstrates why going out with my brother's friends was a mistake in the first place, because it just meant that I didn't want to date someone that could be construed in the back of my mind as a blood relative. Ick. They all felt like brothers. There was one other guy Cole knew named Livingston who was still single, but he was enough of a hot mess, that even I, in the middle of desperate loneliness, knew not to go there.

So yeh, I'd "flown through them all," and it was about five years before the enlistment of Penny and her esteemed, sacred counsel entered my life. Uggggghhhh—I shouldn't have talked to Cole about this! I hung up the phone. It was one of those moments where you bang yourself on the forehead with the butt of your palm going "Stupid stupid stupid" to yourself. I optimistically reasoned there was a chance Cole would forget all about this before mentioning it to Jeannine. One could hope. I did a deep yoga breath: In-through-the-nose.... Ahhhhhh. Now, exhale: Out-through-the mouth. That's better.

So as I mentioned, I had too much time on my hands and needed stuff to do after Stephano and I broke up and taking care of my Dad was one of the ways. I was hanging out at church more too. During that season, I even considered attending the Single's Group, believe it or not, but I felt like that was Burk's region and I didn't want to make him feel awkward. Instead, I volunteered for other ministries like teaching little kids on Sunday mornings and helping make meals for families who needed help because of a new baby or the loss of a loved one. Anywho, because I was around more, I of course ran into Burk more, who, by the way at this point, was WAY more involved at our church than I'd ever been. To think that I'd insinuated he wasn't welcome here just two years earlier? Gheesopete! (Head shaking to right and back again, while lashes are lifted to brows and brows towards infinity, as eyes roll around in my head. I was shocked by my own nerve looking back on it now.)

One day nearing Halloween, I walked out of the children's wing and Burk was walking into a staff member's office. "Hey there," he said with his empathetic smile.

"Hey there," I smiled back.

"How ya doin'?"

"Oh...okay. Stephano and I...we broke up."

"Yeh...I heard about that." He looked sorry. I scrunched up my nose and tried not to be emotional.

"Yeh...it's...hard." I looked off kitty-corner at nothing.

"I know how it must be Rob." Now, I have to say right here that I really appreciated Burk for his willingness in not making me feel bad. He could have said, "Yeh...I KNOW how it feels thanks to you!" while elbowing me with a knowing look. Then, not only would I have been sad, but guilty too. But instead, he chose to return compassion and empathy in the moment and he really didn't have to do it. I still think back to this moment with respect. "Hey," he continued, "you probably know I moved out to the Lakeshore from GR, right? Well, if you ever want to grab coffee just *as friends*, or go for a walk, I'm happy to." And he really said it like he meant it to be just friendship. I looked at him still in such a broken place and said,

"Sure. Maybe I'll take you up on that Burk....sometime..."

"No pressure, okay? I'm here if you need." And then he smiled and walked into the office he was headed to originally. I waved a small hand gesture back,

"See ya. Thanks." It struck me as he had intended it: "I'm your friend." I needed friends, especially if I was going to be a spinster.

Eighteen:
Identity Theft

Well...I guess "identity theft" is one way to describe Halloween, even if it is just stealing an identity for one night of the year. Halloween arrived that year just weeks after the Worst Break-Up of All Time, which was somewhat appropriate since I had never wanted to be another person more than I wanted to that year. In keeping with my luck however, I did not have plans. My roommate Jenny, (who by the way was the only good roommate I'd had since college and who just understood me), had a Halloween party to go to. It was right before my thirty-fourth birthday. She was only twenty-six. I could have been jealous of her youth, but she was the coolest person I'd ever known. But anyway, she had a date, her long time boyfriend Michael, and I had nada. She knew how I felt because being my roommate, she couldn't possibly have missed the drama drama drama and the parade of men that went by her, including Skip, Stephano, the Lug and well Burk? She knew about Burk, but hadn't actually met him I don't think—but no matter, she'd seen enough to know how sad I felt. She knew I was bummed to not have plans.

So, she told me something that kind of cheered me up. She said, "Well...at least you don't have to go to a Halloween party as...FRIAR TUCK!"

"What? You're Friar Tuck?!!"

"Yeh, well Michael is Robin Hood so I'm Friar Tuck..."

"What about Maid Marian?? Or better yet, Guinevere? How could you not be Guinevere, Jen?" [and it was a fair question because she had this crazy gorgeous thick brown hair. It was the kind of hair where one could leave the house with it completely wet, and by mid-morning morning it would dry into cascading perfect curls. Disgusting.] If anyone was Queen Guinevere, it was Jenny!

"Oh well...you know...Karissa got to be Guinevere," she said rolling her eyes. Karissa was Michael's slightly...ahem...eccentric sister. Karissa worked for me once at G. Louise; she was a nice chick for the most part, yet she was really glam so she just managed to get her way about outfits and public appearances, especially if there was a choice between Friar Tuck and Guinevere! And given that Michael's other sister had called dibs on Maid Marian, Jenny explained that she was plum out of King-Arthur babe options. Jenny was so cool that she just rolled her eyes once in private and went with it, making the best of it. Later on in my life, I took a page from her play book: on Halloween one year when I was teaching secondary English Lit and Writing to eleventh and twelfth grade students, I shocked them by borrowing Jeannine's cow costume. I had a reputation, a little bit anyway, for being a cool teacher because I liked fashion...(owning and running a boutique did have a way of leaving a mark on one's ability to put their best fashion foot forward. Fashion is hobby I never outgrew.)

So, I'd prided myself in not wearing Levi bend-over pants to work like many of my unfortunately dressed colleagues. That's how it was, except for Evita, Velma and Estelle who would kill me if I didn't also set them apart from the Levi bend-over panted women. But most of the men wore Dockers. Bend-overs and Dockers were an epidemic in my building. Suffice it to say that when stylish me wore a cow costume, my students came completely unglued: "Ms. BROHHHdie, What are you wearing???!!!," their voices entrenched in shock and dismay. It was tacky and hilarious and slightly unprofessional, yet my students luuuhhhhved that I could be intentionally uncool for one day.

So, I definitely respected this about Jenny, especially on Halloween this year because I needed the laugh. Thanks to having her choices of lovely ladies' costumes gobbled up by her boyfriend's sisters, and, given the pressure of a family-themed Halloween participatory conglomerate, Jenny went to her Halloween party as the ever-so-sexy Friar Tuck. When she walked out the door in her baggy garb, green and brown sack cloth breeches, she held up the head piece and it showed the Friar's bald head with a plastic "comb over" and I almost peed my pants.

So, off Jen went to her party and since I lived in a cute little neighborhood where people up and down the street had little adorable Martha Stewart type carved pumpkins on their porches, I knew there were going to be trick-or-treaters. I locked the front door and turned off all of the lights and planned to hide in the dark from six until eight, because I knew trick-or-treating would be over by then.

But by 7:00, I felt too pathetic, so I called Jeannine and Cole. Jeannine as I mentioned, was on bed rest and they lived in a small rental out in the boonies on the south side of Holland, thirty minutes or so away. Jeannine answered, and explained that they were not having a rip roarin' holiday over there, due to a lack of children bombardment that she had initially calculated—Cole and Jeannine hadn't one trick-or-treater. She explained therefore that she had good news and bad news. The bad news: she was bummed about the lack of fun. The good news: she had a ton of candy and I was more than welcome to come over and help eat it along with Cole and watch a slasher flick.

Well, I didn't like slasher flicks, but you know what they say about desperate times and all...I got a little tired of locking myself up on nights like Halloween because I wasn't willing to be the single girl who lives vicariously through other people's trick-or-treating children, but I also wasn't excited about calling friends at the last minute either. Although my friends were always generous in their willingness to have me over, they were opening up their homes at the last second for me and said things like, "I'm so sorry my house is a mess" and "I'm sorry this is all we have going on..." gesturing to either the extreme quiet due to not having party plans of their own or due to the craziness of kids running to and fro, as if I was entitled to either a lovely party or thoughtful serenity when I called at the last second out of my desperate loneliness. I didn't need or expect a parade in my own honor! I just wanted company. But I sensed it made people feel like they ought to provide one anyway, even though all I wanted was face to face time with people, regardless of whether their house was a mess or not, or there was or wasn't a party. So after much imposition-entrenched companionship (me being the imposition, not them) with family and friends in that season, I decided to give Burk a call.

We started hanging out—but it was infrequent and was above board and he had kept a distance, sticking to his, "just-as-friends" offer. He had offered friendship yes, and it wasn't "a line." He'd meant it. I was downtown Holland almost everyday for classes at Hope College so sometimes in the evenings after he'd finish a workday, we met at J.P.'s. J.P.'s was the original barista in our neck of the woods, before Starbucks popped up on every corner and in every strip mall. It was always there, was always good and is still both! We'd get lattes or chai tea and just talk about light stuff, like the weather, sports, his job, my school stuff, and sometimes faith. He didn't walk me to my car or help me on with my coat and I didn't want him too. We were just friends.

He let me do the calling—let's face it, I'd turned him down for a relationship TWICE, once by breaking up to go back to the Lug and once at the Coffee Grounds in Grand Haven. Wait! Had it been two times or three times? I'd lost count but knew it was enough that he wouldn't initiate time together. So, he let me do the instigating and calling, and I, because of our history, didn't expect it to be otherwise. He was too concerned with his intent being misinterpreted, and I knew that.

But I did think it was odd he was hanging out with me, even on occasion, since a few months prior, he had gone home with Sheila to meet her family in the Chicago area for Thanksgiving. That hadn't been long after our Coffee Grounds'-Grand Haven date, when he'd specifically investigated the prospects of a final chance with me, so he would be able to discern a decision about whether to either move forward with the Sheila-thing, or not. I had assumed they would be engaged soon after, given his clear communication. Yet, over the course of the few months that followed that holiday, I'd heard they'd broken up. I deemed it strange because it seemed that they were two peas in a pod and as much as it had bugged me the year before, even I had to admit that they did seem perfect together. But now he was here having little get-togethers with me and so I finally asked him about it one night when we met for drinks and appetizers for a Friday-happy hour.

"Well," he said, "I just didn't feel like it was going in the right direction. We were too...too...we just weren't getting along." I didn't push for more detail but at least I knew for sure they were over and she wasn't off somewhere being pissed that I was hangin' with her beau, even if we were just friends. I'm just sayin'—it would bug me if my man were hanging out "as friends" with another woman he had previously dated.

One night, a week or so before Christmas, I had just finished exams and was in the mood to celebrate my first long semester being over. I called Burk to see what was up; I hadn't seen him for a couple of weeks anyway. He said he was free if I could go out late. So I met him at our favorite downtown bistro called, "Till Midnight" in Holland. It was a quaint tiny little nook with beautiful art and great wine, just a couple of blocks from the Hope College campus. After a couple of hours of good chat, we left and this time he walked me to my car because it was late and dark. I got in and waved goodbye, but when I went to start the car, my battery was dead! Burk had just pulled out around the corner and I called him on my brand new Qualcomm cell with adjustable antenna: "Burk! Can you come back?? My battery is dead!..." and within seconds he was pulling back in the parking lot. It was almost 11:00 pm and Burk did not have jumper cables and it was too late to call a friend who might, so he took me all the way home to Grand Haven—a 70 minute round-trip drive for him.

I had figured that I'd just call Cole to help me get my car jumped and back up running tomorrow. But it was thoughtful of Burk to not only take me home, but I also noticed that he didn't overplay it—he just dropped me off, made sure the door shut safely behind me and waved "goodnight" as if he were one of my friend's parents dropping me off when I was fourteen.

After all of this, I was absolutely convinced that Burk did not have romantic feelings for me....which was fine. I wasn't in a place to receive that even if he'd had them. You have to understand that Burk was a person, who in the past would ingest too much wine on purpose when over at my house and exclaim that it was now unsafe that he drive home to Grand Rapids, so could he just stay on the couch. "Well...looky there...the bottle is empty.....too bad I can't drive myself home now... guess I'll just have to stay!" I fell for it the first time but later realized he was doing it on purpose so he could just hang out with me longer. In the past, Burk had not been one to misuse an opportunity like this dead-battery thing, so that's why I was certain he was over me too.

Nineteen:
A New Year

For the past several Christmases, I had spent much of the holiday by myself—it was alright since several years earlier I had determined that I'd had it with the "Aunts'" and many other relatives, sharing their comments that drew attention to the state of my singleness. I mean, why do we have to talk about singleness? I felt like it should be a protected category like for example, age discrimination in the workplace (if you're over forty, you're in a protected category which means if your boss needs to fire you, it better be because you suck at your job, not because you're over forty and he/she can hire someone half your age at half the price.) In keeping with age discrimination then, we've also learned it isn't polite to ask someone's age once they turn....oh about forty. One is a violation of a legal protection and the other one is just plain old-fashioned good manners. My aunts did not have good manners. Ya know my Mom's art for being direct, combined with a lack in political correctness? Yeh well...it kind of runs in the family and there are six of them in addition to her! Six German aunts and uncles. If singleness could be thought of as something that didn't make a person an "enigma," and if I could just be considered someone who *happened* to be single like three of them *happened* to be divorced, or like one of them *happened* to be bad at make-up application, or such as all five sisters *happened* to be the embodiment of bouffant hairdos that had gone out of style twenty-five years prior, well then...I would go to the monstrosity of a Christmas party at my Aunt Bonnie's house. But they couldn't help themselves from singling out my singleness and so I'd chosen to no longer be exposed [...although, I promised myself that if I ever changed my mind, then the next time I were to attend, I would certainly bring along photographs of Jennifer Aniston as a visual aid for in-style hair. I would make these into laminate flashcards for my aunts to use as an easy reference.]

As a family, my brothers and their wives/girlfriends would all gather for gift giving on Christmas morning and then about noon, we would part ways, Cole and Jeannine racing off to Indiana to spend the rest of the day with her mom, and my parents traversing over to Belding to Aunt Bonnie's. I, on the the other hand, would sit on their couch (instead of my own because they had elaborate Christmas decorations and it made me feel Christmassy and less alone) and watch *Peanuts' Christmas, It's a Wonderful Life*, and Dickins', *Christmas Carol* along with a bottle of Chardonnay and my Cocker Spaniel, Vic. When this afternoon Christmas would begin, I used to cry because it felt pathetic. Yet as the years went by, I began to look forward to it because it eventually became my own little tradition.

Now, you are wondering: what about all of those dudes you dated and why didn't you spend any Christmases with any of them? Well, the Christmases I'm referring to were the last few I was on and off with the Lug (because it seemed, we were always "off" at Christmas—it figures doesn't it??) There were also a few Christmases after the Lug it turned out that my only alternative for company on Christmas Day was Aunt Bon's party. I'd finally managed to break it off with the Lug for good early in 1999. But it was a few years prior that this lonely Christmas ritual had begun.

It turns out that Nineteen Ninety-Nine didn't make me want to party necessarily just as Prince had boldly suggested I would, since it was the year in which I'd met Stephano, fell madly in love only to have it swept away like a giant stage hook. Being alone this Christmas was definitely a surprise: I'd spent most of the year assuming I'd spend it with the Ferrante family. As early as September, I'd been satisfied by the conclusion that this year finally, it would be a fine holiday because I wouldn't be stuck alone on Christmas. Hence, Vic, my spaniel who had ears so long he stepped on them when he went out in the snow, would, once he'd thaw out, sit next to me on the couch. As if to take my face in his paws, he would look at me with knowing brown eyes that said, "I know it. I knowwwww Honey. I just know." So, this dog and me were tight.

But I remembered that this was the year I'd taken stock of my life and had chosen to manually move the items in the blessings' category ahead of the grouping in the disappointments' column. I was used to this little Christmas ritual after all, and the idea of maxin' and relaxin' with Vic and watching movies far outweighed the big Brock-family Christmas party and being confronted with uncomfortable remarks. So in that light, I actually began to see this afternoon holiday tradition as a blessing. A cozy atmosphere, a fuzzy adoring dog, a blanket and of course, Chardonnay. I could still afford to buy wine—talk about a relief?! So that year, I turned what had become an annual unwanted custom, into a mini celebration, drinking wine out of one of the crystal wine goblets that Nate had given me a couple of years prior. Why not? So what if he'd given me an inappropriately expensive gift, bless-his-heart? There was no harm in using them for their intended purpose! Can I get a knuckle-bump? Just sayin'.

Christmas hadn't been the best season for me up until then for more than one reason though. See, and you thought I was going to blame it all on the Aunts! Nahhh. They did exacerbate some feelings for me that time of year but here's why I was plum ripe to be exacerbated in the first place: years before, somewhere around 1996, the Lug had given me a diamond ring on a wind whipping shoreline in

Muskegon. We'd been dating for five years. I was 30 years old. He was 36. We were none too young for this important step. For a long time prior to this proposal, he had teased me about getting engaged, which helped to bribe me into going on a trip to Las Vegas along with he and another couple. I guess the other couple's presence was supposed to ensure my conviction that he was not, in fact, commitment phobic. 'Sounds like it would be a great engagement story, right? Hey Everyone, guess what?!! I got engaged in Vegas!

Guess what I did? You're shocked, right, that I fell for this and went to Vegas? Guess what else? He put the ring in its black little velvet box, and placed it right on the security conveyor belt, all by ITSELF and sent it through security as it's own entity. He did not place it discreetly in a bag or a coat pocket. This was before September eleventh, of 2001: airport security didn't make you take off your coat and shoes back then. They did not neither, wave a wand-reader over your private undergarments. [I have a friend who recently received a full-fledged mammogram while we were traveling from Houston to Grand Rapids by a border agent as we were exiting Mexico. Poor Gabrielle was the unlucky one of the two of us. I had only received the stop-and-frisk. This ring incident was prior to airport security mammograms.] The Lug could have chosen to place the ring box *in his pocket* and no one would have thought anything about it back then, unless it had been made of titanium, WHICH it was not.

Let me ask you another question. There is a fruit basket waiting for you if you answer correctly:

Do you think I got engaged to the Lug in Vegas?

Ding ding ding ding ding! You just won a fruit basket!!! Of course I didn't get engaged in Vegas. He wasn't even close to asking me but he hung the idea out there complete with a diamond ring like it would happen, as if it had its own plane ticket and was securely buckled into a plane seat, with a puke bag tucked into the seat pocket in front of him. Her? (What gender do we ascribe to a personified ring?)

But on this Muskegon Shoreline Christmas Eve in 1996 at 5:00 pm with the wind whipping out of the north, he finally gave me the ring in question and said, "Let's be together." He didn't get down on one knee, but I excused it because it was nineteen degrees.

Still, I was flipping out! Given everything, you can imagine I wasn't completely surprised by the proposal—I had been having the "now or never" talk with him for awhile. But I was excited nonetheless. I had gotten engaged on Christmas Eve! As I climbed back into Lug's beamer grateful to be out of the wind, I thought, "Whew—everything we've been through up until now has just been 'growing pains.' Now we're sure of each other and on track!" We rushed home because I had to sing in church, drive back south to Grand Haven, and then drive all of the way to Holland to get to church—Lug was meeting me there and so it was a whirlwind. Of course I called everybody in the few minutes I had at home to change and say, "I'm ENGAGED!" So, by the time I got to church two hours later, it had spread like wildfire and women I'd never even met were asking me if they could see the ring. (It was a stunning 1.5 carats in a platinum setting, although not a complete surprise mind you, because I had seen it before when it went through security at the airport that one time.) Believe it or not, it did occur to me a striking notification about myself...that I really didn't care about the ring so much...I realized this as I first began extending my hand to show it as others asked to see it....it made me feel uncomfortable flashing it around to people I hardly knew. It seemed to mean more to him than it did to me, because I'd concluded that in his mind at least, the ring itself was the glue that guaranteed that the commitment would stick.

After the service, we stopped at my parents' for a little Christmas celebration, and then off to midnight Mass at the Lug's church and by the time we got there, his entire family knew too.

His sisters were hugging me but Carrie, the Lug's youngest sister, had this look in her eye, like, "I hope you know what you're doing..." She loved her brother, but she knew he was dark and hard to pin down. She liked me a lot, so she was always honest with me about what she thought. Her look standing there in the vestibule of the church, said, "I'd be careful if I were you" or maybe it said "Don't count on it..." But I definitely saw concern. No matter. Onto kissing and hugging the rest of his family! The 1.5 carat ring had inoculated me against negativity. We were official. Finally!

It was a late night and we finally went to bed somewhere after 2:30 am. Four hours later I awoke to go to the traditional Christmas morning at my Mom's and assumed of course that my new fiancé was coming. He seemed cold and distant...again. As the person I was who could not allow one nonverbal cue to go by without hooking on it, I turned to him and said, "We're engaged! Aren't you happy? What's wrong??" I gave him a side arm shrug hug.

"I dunno. Just tired I guess." I was irritated because it was my first Christmas as a bride-to-be. So I tried to get him in the Christmas spirit: in a festive manner I asked him,

"Well, let's talk about wedding dates....When do you want to get married?? Do you want to get married at Christmas next year??" He looked at me like, "Please. I haven't had my coffee yet." Suddenly, fear blanketed itself over me with a side of dread attached and I started backing away from him. "We are getting married, right? You wouldn't have given me this ring..." I looked at my left hand and held it up, shaking, "Ya...You wouldn't have given me this ring if...if...you didn't mean to say we were getting married?!"

"I think we'll eventually get married, Robbi. But why do we have to set a date right now? Why can't we just *enjoy being engaged for awhile?*" [emphasis mine].

I was starting to tear up. Stammering, "..be...beh...because of everything we've been through....because of five years of Cat and Mouse...because you've made a hundred promises you haven't kept. You wouldn't do this to me now, right? You wouldn't give me a ring, let me tell everyone we're engaged and then not expect to follow through??" I was now exasperated. It was 7:25 am on Christmas morning; I had been engaged for fourteen hours and twenty-five minutes.

"Rob, I said we'd set a date eventually! I don't wanna discuss it anymore!" And just like that he stormed off to get his coffee. I was horrified. I drove home before going to my Mom's. I called her and it was now almost 8 in the morning, a mere 15 hours had passed since I'd gotten engaged on Christmas Eve. I called her and I was clearly crying and upset, yet unwilling to tell her what had really happened. I couldn't bear the truth being out there after I'd paraded my news around (like any newly engaged chick might do, but still—I was SO embarrassed, ashamed and disappointed). So I made up some story about something happening on his side of the family and that I wasn't myself, and yes I was crying, but I'd eventually be fine and over to her house. She tried to coax it out of me but I simply was not going to tell her, while apologizing that the Lug would not be coming over due to his "family incident"...whatever it was.

I finally arrived with tired swollen eyes. I had tried to reduce the swelling by placing ice packs on my face before I got to my parents' house, but to no avail—it had only served to make them redder. So, it was a stressful morning of unwrapping gifts while I kept trying to tell Jeannine and Deborah that I "couldn't talk about it." They knew me too well—they knew the situation too well. They were pissed at the Lug because they figured he'd done something, they just didn't know what exactly. But I didn't want to ruin anyone's Christmas.

And THAT my Dear Readers, is how the Christmas afternoon tradition of watching movies along with only a couch, a dog, a movie and Chardonnay began. I didn't speak to the Lug for a couple of days.

'Didn't show up. 'Didn't answer the phone. And tried not to be home so he wouldn't find me if he came looking.

And this was only the *first* time he gave me that engagement ring and didn't mean it.

So, here I was now, four Christmases later, sipping Chard and watching Linus tell the Christmas story while looking at Vic. "It's just you and me, Dude." My thirty-fourth birthday had been the month before and it does make a girl wonder how many more Christmases would be spent alone. But remember what I told you about my epiphany and how I was going to view my life after Stephano had left? Remember how I'd chosen to look down a path of hope instead of negativity? (... even if the hope was hanging over my toilet?) This was a good opportunity to again ascertain points of gratitude instead of issues of loss. So, curled up on a leather sofa in front of the Christmas tree in a hand-knit afghan and snuggling Vic, I did a mental checklist:

#1

—I'd recently been hangin' out with Burk and I felt that having his friendship was good company. I had bought him a little Christmas present to give later on—he was out in Massachusetts with his fam. I was kind of looking forward to his return.

#2

—And Jeannine was enormously pregnant now (I don't think she was counting the enormous part as a "blessing" but I did because it meant the baby was still in there!) The miracle child was due the first week of February and I was so thankful, because even if she had been born now (we knew it was a "she"), not only would she be viable, but strong! The doctors gave Jeannine and Cole every assurance that from here on out, it was a normal pregnancy.

#3

—I'd just finished my first semester back in college and had gotten straight A's. Even though earlier in my life I had earned accomplishments like recording an entire cd, having my songs played on the radio, and having sung at events with thousands of people in attendance, still ...this was the strongest feeling of accomplishment I'd ever experienced. The first time I'd been to college, I'd kind of skated through, settling for low B's and C's because I didn't see myself as an academic; I saw myself as a musician. My music classes were the only ones in which I worked for A's. It turned out that I was smart, and I'd just found this out for the first time a few days ago when my report card was issued. Huh. Me, an "A" student. Who knew?! It was a pretty great feeling, running to my front door when I heard the mailman drop the stack through the front-door slat, to reach down, haphazardly flip through the mess on the floor and find it, tear off the perforated end of that little carbonized mailing and see a column with straight A's down the right side for the first time in my life! Think of it: I already had a BA degree. I'd opened up many a report card in my day and I'd had never seen a column like that one. It was the best Christmas present ever, because I'd given it to myself. No lights. No camera. No action. No high heels. No make-up. No one watching. None of my professors even conferring with one another. There was no committee of "they" labeling me successful: just freakin' hard work and something tangible to show for it. I more than liked the feeling. It was certainly better than a pretend engagement.

So, that's a nice list of thankful items, right, in spite of being alone on Christmas?! I had some other friends in the room now besides Vic and Linus. Their names were Self-worth and Self-respect. Self-loathing hadn't bothered to come this year. Self-pity must have been out sick because it hadn't shown up either.

This Christmas I wasn't drowning in pain and loss as in Christmases past like when I'd gotten engaged on Christmas Eve and unengaged by Christmas morning. I was actually *celebrating* Christmas, even though I was by myself. True, I did miss Stephano a little and wondered how his Christmas was going. He'd told me all about how his family celebrates Christmas when he was convinced we would be spending it together; I thought through some of the details he'd shared and hoped it was merry. I wished I would have maybe heard something from him—a card, perhaps, as it had only been about two months since our break up. I still held onto a little bit of hope for him, because I wasn't convinced in my conscious mind yet, what my unconscious heart already knew, that I wouldn't have ultimately been happy with him over the long term. Yet, this was a place of contemplative sadness, not the kind that makes you want to heave with angst, or as Lizzy's husband Joe put it, gave you "the crazies." Have you ever had the crazies? The crazies suck. It was another tangible point of gratitude: I was over "the crazies." Merry Christmas to me, I warmly thought. Some people dream of engagement rings or velvet boxes with some kind of a treasure inside—some people long for the latest "it" toy or the perfect, albeit fictional, never-happening gift, but I felt gifted and blessed just to have "the crazies" behind me. No more crazies from Stephano. No more crazies from the Lug. [Literally AND figuratively. Pun absolutely intended.]

It was almost a New Year. I had a different type of hope for the coming year. In New Years' past I didn't have much hope; I felt hopeless when the old year had ticked over to the new, because I didn't view anything changing for the better going forward, either for my singleness or for my professional identity. In New Years' past, I was a chick that failed at pageants and a music career and owning a boutique, and who was a marginal student who couldn't get the guy she loved to marry her; therefore, I asked questions like: what on earth was I going to do with my life? It seems funny now and it kind of is in more ways than one. It's funny I ever thought pageants were a justifiable means to an end for me; funny I was the last to know that I was smart! 'Funny that I believed on some level that around the age of thirty, I was washed up and had no other talents or gifts that God could drag out of me; funny that I couldn't see there was a life beyond any of my mistakes or failures.

But this hope I now had was a hope that was in the process of creating something from its own wreck. In fact, it wasn't just hope— it was peace. I had the peace that passes understanding. Have you ever felt that in spite of the circumstances around you which clearly dictate you should feel anything but peace, that peace can still be experienced? I think I just finally got tired of feeling like a victim and therefore being one. Being in school gave me some peace for my professional life because I would have a tangible, marketable skill that I could pay my bills with, even though I could have been focused on, "What if I can't get a job when I'm done? What if I never pay off my debt? What if Amway would have worked out better than this supposed teaching thing? What if my music career had taken off?" But the what-iffing is a peace grabber. And at least for this coming New Year, I had pretty much decided the peace grabber was absent and that I was Teflon. It was one of the few seasons in my life where I finally knew what that Biblical phrase from Proverbs means—I could finally put empathy to it. The peace that passes understanding. Hello 2000! I'm not sure what you have in store, but I know it's going to be better than '99,' 98' 97' and well...my whole life up until this point.

Twenty:
Leap Year

The new year came along with a new semester of school for me. I went out the first weekend in January with Burk, just to toast in the New Year (a week late) and give him a belated Christmas present, which was a cobalt-blue lead crystal votive holder. Burk liked that color blue and he liked little nick-nacky effects. He was actually minimalistic in his collection of them, but he had good taste. He was also an historian, so understood what artifacts were. My point: he was good at being nick nacky, which I don't think most people are. Now I suppose this is a strange quality to admire in a person. Can you imagine: one gossipy friend to another, whispering a question, "What does she see in him?"

The other girl's response: "She thinks he's a good Nick-Nacker."

I'm just supposing Burk would have preferred to be known for some other attribute that was fairly more sexy. But it was what I thought when I saw the candle holder, so I bought it for him. At least he didn't get stale cookies as did Nate. Or a pretend engagement diamond as had I. And besides, when I first went to Burk's place for the first time and was taking in the atmosphere, he said, "I like the messy library look," so I knew he'd like it and I also knew it would go in his house. Not surprisingly, he did not get me a present, given the wine topper vs. ceramic vase debacle of New Year's 1998. I wasn't expecting anything: we were just friends. My gift to him was just something I happened to walk by in a department store; it caught my eye, which is the vein in which I gave it.

Meanwhile back at the ranch, we were all on pins and needles wondering when Talia would be born. Much to Jeannine's chagrin, after all that with the bed rest and the magnesium sulfate and the extended hospital stays and the steroids, her pregnancy went complete and utter full term, which I guess is the point as to why she had to do all of that. The prescription for not losing her baby had worked. But near the end there, as all 38/39 week pregnant women do, Jeannine was hoping to begin contractions a week earlier anyway. She was saying things like, "Could we just get the bowling ball off of my pelvis for the love of MIKE!" And, "Get. It. Out. Of. ME!!"

"It" finally came on February 4th and I never felt so much love in my heart for anyone or anything before: I stared down at her all swaddled up like a burrito with a pink chef's hat (that Jeannine's mom bought) and her little baby love reached back to me. This beautiful moment was happening simultaneously despite the fact that upon my arrival to the hospital room, Jeannine, exactly seventy-five minutes post-labor, was wolfing down a Wendy's Single with cheese. "I'm just a little hungry, Dudes." It struck me as hilarious to see a woman who'd just been through an arduous delivery acting somehow like herself! But what did I know. Maybe you did? Maybe one does? Who knows.

I was a little mad when my time to hold Talia was up, because I felt like I could have nuzzled her for a lifetime—which would probably be weird by the time she was fourteen. Still, in this case the cliché is appropriate. I did feel like that. But then so did everyone else in the room (except for the nurse perhaps) because Talia was the first grandchild on both sides of the family. Cole was beaming like a single lamppost in the dead of night and both Grandmas already wanted a second turn. Let's face it: I was way down the pecking order for Talia time.

So that night I prayed for my newly born niece for the first time outside of the womb. I cried myself to sleep with happy tears.

A week after Talia was born, I flew out to Marathon Key. My half sister Iris, had a winter condo down there with her husband Toby. They were going to be gone for a few days and needed a dog sitter. Hmmm. Allow me to consider for a moment.... Florida in February and all I have to do is sit with your Miniature Schnauzer, Zeus? All three pounds of him? And I'm broke, so...I wouldn't be taking this trip otherwise? Boy, give me one second (one, literally) to think about that?! And so of course I went, especially since it lined right up with my winter break.

I had called Burk the day after Talia was born to tell him the great news. He was flying out also, to India. He was going for the second year in a row with a group from church. "How did you manage to get two weeks off from work?" I remembered he'd gone on this same trip last year, but things had really heated up with his job in the past twelve months, so I was a little surprised he could go this year, since it seemed like all Burk did was work.

"Because you know, Robyn, all I do is work—I never take any other time off and I haven't since I went last year."

"You wouldn't take time off anyway."

"Yeh...yeh...and I know they'd rather I spread the two weeks of 'vacation' over the course of the year a little more, but since this trip is pro bono work for a charitable cause, they're willing to work with me..." Burk was an associate firm-lawyer and was therefore at the bottom of the food chain. He worked from 6 am until 10 pm every single workday and usually put in a full eight hours on Saturdays too. Sundays he usually took off, but that was it. I figured when he got home from his trip, he was going to need a vacation from his vacation. But whatever, he flew out on February fifth. And I left on the ninth for Marathon.

For five days I had no distractions. I had never been to my sister's Florida place before: her condo overlooked the ocean and they were on the second floor. From their balcony, you could throw a rock and hit the water's edge. It was a perfect paradise. Besides taking Zeus on a few daily walks, it was just Zeus, the ocean, a few movie rentals and me. I had a lot of time to think. Now, let's pause a moment and let me ask you a little question:

Do you think I'm much of a thinker? Bahahahahahaha! For cryin' out loud, I wish I could turn my thinker OFF sometimes, but I couldn't so I didn't. I analyzed my life—took in all of its blessings: I accepted that I no longer missed Stephano, although I did miss my baby niece, but she was a sure thing the second I got back. I thought about my new career as a high school English teacher and how, despite the gargantuan amount of work, how much I absolutely loved it. And by the way, if you'e out there and one part of you thinks that you're too old to change your career? That is a lie! In fact, my sister for whom I was dog sitting, had gone back to school herself, just a few years prior to get her certification as a Psychotherapist. She already had a Bachelor of Music degree in Classical Piano. But because she wanted to do counseling, she had to take a bunch of undergrad prerequisites prior to even starting grad school and that part took a couple of years: *then* she earned her Masters after that and at the age of fifty-eight, graduated and began a new career in family counseling. She had inspired me, and frankly her example took away my excuses not to go back. I was just a baby at thirty-four to be back in school!

I do think it's great if a young person knows what to do with the rest of their life when they graduate from high school at the ripe age of eighteen, go to college for four or five years and then begin working in that chosen field. But not everybody figures it out by that age. It almost seems like a far-fetched idea, that by eighteen you're supposed to know everything you're supposed to know. It doesn't even sound rational! Many people do it that way and good for them. But I'm just sayin'—you are never to old to reinvent yourself!

So where was I? Oh yeh—taking stock of my present life on a condo balcony overlooking the beach in Marathon Key. It was a clear night, the moon was shining on the water, its reflection spreading itself out in a long shiny stripe of gold on a blackish purple ocean's surface. As I thought about everything, my mind wandered over to Burk; I wondered about how he was doing in India, going there to help facilitate an annual conference for a man by the name of Yesu who lived in Vijayawada. Burk helped with administrative stuff and frankly whatever needed to be done. India was a really long way away. "I hope he's ok," I thought to myself. And then it subtly poked me on the shoulder—this awareness that I actually missed Burk. It didn't hit me like a ton of bricks, it rather poked me on the shoulder in a whisper like, "Hey, I think you maybe sorta like him—I think you maybe sorta miss him...."

I talked back to it: That's ridiculous! I pushed it out of my mind.

Then a minute later: Maybe I do??

Ten seconds after that: Naw! Couldn't be. No way.

With that I went to bed. I figured going to sleep was the one sure way to not have to think about it anymore that night.

And then I woke up with Zeus snoring at the end of the bed at 7:00 am; it was still there. I missed Burk. I was worried about Burk. Burk was more than a friend to me. This was before Facebook and before people had email on their cell phones. I had absolutely no way to contact Burk to even see how he was doing. And besides, I wasn't overly comfortable with my epiphanic findings. I needed to let it percolate for a few days anyway, but I am just telling you that if there had been Facebook messaging or if he'd had cell service over there, I absolutely would have sent him an email just to say, "Hi," and to "check on him." [Sidebar: Clearly I had feelings for him because I am not typically a checker-onner with members of the opposite sex who I claim are "just friends." Remember Nate and Iowa?]

I flew home the day after that and had successfully pushed my realization to the back burner since I had school the next day, and Burk wasn't even home for at least two more days. I had essays to edit, chapters to finish, and projects to focus on, and of course, a baby niece to hold!

A couple of days later though, I was in full school start-up mode. I knew Burk had been home for a day or so. I left him a voicemail just saying I hoped he had a good trip and I surmised he was resting up (due to the 14-hour time difference). I didn't hear anything from him that Monday night and I didn't really expect to. But the next day, I was racing around to get out the door for a 4 o'clock class, when the phone rang. It was presently 3:15 and it took me thirty minutes to get to campus. But I grabbed the phone and checked it. It was Burk:

"Hello?!" (I was trying not to sound excited.)

"Hi Rob—Hey, I got your message. This is my first day back in the office and I was sleeping all day when you called yesterday—sorry I missed you!"

"You sound great! You must have had an amazing trip!"

"Yeh, I did—it was very different this year than last, but I will explain what I mean about that later. Hey,...uh...speaking of later, what are you doing tonight? Can you have dinner??" Okay, I was really excited about seeing Burk and at the prospect of having dinner, but I had to leave in five minuets and I looked down at my outfit: I was wearing yellow denim J. Crew overalls. Holy Crap—I couldn't go straight from my two-hour seminar class to dinner with Burk wearing this! And I also had a mountain of homework. With hesitation in my voice, I said,

"Oh my gosh, I would love to see you...I...well...I have homework... and I should do it...and—"

"Blow it off Rob. Come out to dinner with me!"

I began a quick mental reasoning out checklist that I actually could probably make it if I drove home to change and do my hair before I met up with him, so I said, "Okay. Let's do it, but can you do it late?? Can you do...like 7:30??" Dudes—I was not one to blow off homework. This was big.

"Sure, I have to drive home from GR anyway, so can meet you at my place on the Lakeshore at 7:20/7:30?"

"Perfect! Gotta go—see you then!" I raced out the door, jumped in my red Jetta, buckled my seat belt, popped the top of my diet coke can and took a slug, slammed it in the cup-holder, dialed Jeannine, pulled out of the driveway and I talked to her all the way to class.

I told Jeannine: "Okay, what if I told you I kind of think I might have feelings...like...THOSE kind of feelings...for Burk?"

"Oh my gosh oh my gosh oh my gosh! Wow. Okay...just sec—let me get Talia's binky." I could hear my sweet baby niece making noises like she needed to eat. "Okay, there—this should hold her off for about three minutes. So why do you think that? Like how do you know??" Then I explained how it had just come over me over the course of time but that I absolutely knew that I wanted to date him again. And then I told her how I had an impromptu date with him in just three and a half hours, while spewing out a question, So whadda I do? Do I tell him about my feelings?—Do I hope he guesses? Do I—"

"Rob, no you can't tell him. We just have to hope that it comes up. He's the one that has to bring it up because he's asked you to be with him three separate times and you've said 'no' to him three separate times. No way—if you want to be one-hundred-percent believed, then he has to be the one who brings it up." I figured she might be right. Let's see: I broke up with Burk two years prior to now right before Christmas, after the drunken church incident, and then again when he brought me back that gift from Massachusetts. Then I told him "no" a year ago when he asked me to have that coffee before he and "Sheila took things to the next level." Nah—I couldn't be the one to bring it up. "But Jeannie, what if he never brings it up?"

"Well, I guess you'd have to eventually, like in a few months, but Rob it's better if *he* brings it up to you because then you'll both have more trust that it's real." Right again, Jeannine. I was going with it because regardless of the score I kept in my head about her wisdom regarding my dating life, she'd bore witness to ALL of it, so she kind of had a right to have an opinion...aside from the obvious fact that I'd asked her opinion.

Jeannine at this point, had been married to my brother for four years. But for the ten before that, we'd been friends and even lived together for two years in a condo. She worked for me at my store as well and then, through a series of ridiculously strange events, we'd lived at my parents house together: Jeannine, Cole, my parents, Cole's friend Bobby, me, a bulldog and a cocker spaniel all lived at my parents' place at the same time, and Jeannine and I in the same room! Suffice it to say, she was privy to a great deal of info about my love life, being a fourteen-year witness. I trusted her. Remember how Cole didn't like any of the boyfriends, well except for Skip? Remember how he took painstakingly intense moves to subtly help along some of those break ups? Well, not with Burk! Jeannine and Cole both LOVED Burk, and although Jeannine had been a little more generous and open-minded about the other men, Cole had not. So usually he wasn't the first to know the details of what was going on in my love-life, although he kept up on the themes of it. Jeannine was. And anyway, how weird would it have been anyway for me to confide in Cole with dating details:

"Oh my gosh, okay, so....I walked into the room....and then he walked into the room...and then ...[I've already lost Cole, who by now would be tinkering with his laptop or the stereo dial in his car...] and this guy was wearing the cutest red shirt and it made him look so handsome and I hoped all evening long that he would kiss me and then??? Then he kissed me!!!!"

Can you imagine Cole sitting through that and actually caring? If he wasn't puking, he'd at least be rolling his eyes as if to say, "Puuuhhhlease ask me if I care?!" No chance, so sisters don't tell brothers that stuff. Sisters tell sisters that stuff and Jeannine was the closest thing I had to a full-fledged sis. Yes, I know I mentioned my three half sisters but we weren't girlfriend-close because they were between twenty and thirty years older than me and were spread all over the country. Bringing them into dating details would have been like telling my Mom. I did hit them with the high points on occasion... like I did with my own Mom, but they weren't my go-to confidants [although absolutely all of them had hoped and prayed I wouldn't marry the Lug].

So, Cole liked Burk—Jeannine like Burk. And I would later on find out that while I was driving to class, Cole had come in from work and Jeannine was mouthing the general bullet points to him and he was doin' a happy dance all around the living room. Jeannine said later she was not physically doing the happy dance since she was lactating and all, but she explained she was doing it in spirit!

I told her I had to go because class was starting in five minutes and I needed two hands to park and grab my backpack. She said, "Okay: good luck! Tell me what happens as soon as you can and remember, let HIM bring it up. That's what I'm hoping for!"

"Me too Sister, me too!" And off I went to class, completely distracted from my "Teaching English in the Secondary Classroom" seminar. All I could think about was that I had only thirty minutes to get home...only thirty minutes to transform myself into a sexy looking goddess (a far cry from the way I presently looked—did I mention the yellow denim overalls? I know for sure I didn't tell you about the ponytail or the minimal make up...) THEN, I only had thirty more minutes to turn around, drive back to Holland to make it to Burk's pretending that I always looked this hot. *Yeh Burk, I am a smokin' hot babe when I go to class—I got dressed like this at 6:00 am and here I am on your doorstep still looking as fresh as a daisy!*

Now, one might ask why for goodness sake I didn't ask him to just drive up to Grand Haven? It's because I wanted to be comfortable and familiar. Burk and I had spent a lot more time hanging out in Holland, especially downtown; their coffee shops and restaurants were friendly to us (...at least they were to me). Remember how when I was entrapped in Skip's car, coming home for the family reunion and I befriended all of the familiar landmarks, including the fast food establishments and gas stations? This was similar. I wanted it to be "easy" for us—not awkward. Since I KNEW I was feeling different about him, I was already so nervous.

So, I mustered up some gaul and asked Dr. Moltson if I could leave a few minutes early due to "...an unexpected circumstance." I inwardly laughed at my own choice of words: unexpected circumstance? What Robyn, do you have to do...in one hour and fifty minutes instead of one hour and sixty minutes?? Ummmm: See here, Dr. Moltson?! I think I'm unexpectedly in love and am un-ex-SPECT-did-ly seeing him tonight and I'm wearing overalls, you see? And well that's a little bit of a problem because it isn't good enough and well...you understand, don't you?

Ladies and Gents, let me tell you something: I was a straight-A student. I was not used to telling fibs to teachers or asking for special favors. This was a second chance at a career so I just always showed up, prepared for more than what was expected and did what I was told. Excuses were for amateurs, which I used to be when it came to school. I'd put my time in as an amateur. So fortunately because that was my usual vibe, he looked at me with an empathetic smile and said, "Ya know what? Tonight's a good night for you to sneak out a few minutes early. In fact, I think I'll let everyone go a few minutes early."

See? This Burk thing was going to work because the gods were already smiling down on it through my schedule, given my special-favor amateurish request, because its good-will had trickled over to everybody else in the class. So at 5:45, I was outta there and racing back north up US 31.

I got home, ran in the front door and took the stairs two at a time. I ran in the bathroom and furiously sprayed water into my hair to to get the ponytail-bump line out of the back and ferociously blew it dry, as though my being in a panic would give the hairdryer more watts. I blew heat into three round brushes I left on top of my head and ran into the bedroom. I rushed around throwing things out of the closet and onto the bed, trying to find an outfit that didn't say: I have no interest in ever dating you but that also didn't look like was trying too hard, and yet didn't look like I was trying to say, "Yes Burk, I am a sex kitten and I am madly in love with you." I wanted subtle and a little romantic, but not blatantly obvious. Geesh—as if I've had NO practice in preparing my outfit for a date with a guy I liked. Talk about not being an amateur at something?! As you now know, I'd been in EVERY imaginable situation and so I needed to calm down and breathe deeply and go on my instincts. Okay—I need to breathe in through the nose and out through the mouth in a calm and organized fashion. Whew. Okay. I found my breath and my tan crepe trousers, a fitted blouse and a rockin' belt. I touched up my make up, pieced my hair out and in a cloud of hairspray declared it "Finis'." I finally got out of there in 35 minutes. It was 7:05. I glanced in my rear view. Pretty good for a 35-minute makeover.

I don't remember having one lucid thought on the way to Burk's except that I saw the world differently now that I "liked" him. I hadn't seen him since the first week of January outside of running into him at church, so it was all very new to me—seeing him as a guy I had a crush on. I'd seen him a million times as a friend, but not like this since our brief dating stint more than two years before. Even so, seeing him in a romantic light meant more now than it did then, because we had a history between us. I pulled onto Burk's street and he was at the door the second I got there. He opened it before I knocked and said, "You look great! I like your short hair?! When did you get it cut?" Oh that's right, he hadn't seen me since I got the inverted bob.

"About a month ago—"

"It's cute!...oh come on in, I was just grabbing my keys..." So I followed him in and went right back out again to get into the Ford Explorer. We drove downtown to 'Till Midnight. It was the twenty-ninth of February. The host sat us at a little table by the front window and while we were looking at the menu, Burk started what I suspected might be flirting with me?? He was holding the menu in front of him like he was reading it but then peeked out from behind and smiled at me—it was a little like a clown face. Then he did it again on the other side of the menu. He was being a goofball, so I couldn't tell if he was actually flirting or just still adjusting to Eastern Standard Time— Maybe this was just slap-happiness from jet lag.

Burk ordered a gin and tonic and I had a glass of _ _ _ _ _ _ _ _ _ _.
fill in the blank

[Since you are a Loyal Reader by this point of my story, I refuse to insult your intelligence by telling you what I ordered to drink! I honor your reading comprehension.] When the server brought our drinks, I settled down a little bit. I asked him about India. He nodded towards his short tumbler with the G&T and explained that he better drink it slowly because it was his first drink in sixty days. "Sixty days? Not even a beer in sixty days?" He shrugged his shoulders and said he was trying to concentrate on the trip itself because he was going there to do something important; he said he was trying to focus on the task for the greater good, rather on himself. He said, "It was kind of like a fast, I guess. Every time I had an urge for a beer or a drink, I tried to think about the work I was going to do instead..." I was thinking, "Well—for goodness sake, slam that drink because means it will take effect quickly and then I won't be so nervous!"

Before the server came back to take our food order, he said, "Rob, I have to tell you something..." I remember this moment so well because we were both still holding those enormous menus and the table was tiny and he was about to say something important—where does one negotiate placing a menu that was 18 inches tall, especially when there were two of them? Burk didn't care. He forged ahead: "Rob...I've been thinking a lot, especially on this trip...and I wanted to ask you something...." My knee was bouncing under the table. My face was trying to appear normal, whatever that means. Burke continued, "...I know I've asked you this before but the past few months have seemed... well different...and I guess I was wondering if you wanted to date me again? I want more with you Robyn. I want to give 'us' a shot. I want to start out today exclusively dating you. I don't want to mess around and play games and do all of that unnecessary hoop jumping. I want a real chance for 'us.'"

My knee was bouncing faster now. "Burk, me too. I was hoping we could have this talk tonight. I never would have brought it up to you though because of the past, because of all of the times I've hurt you by saying, 'no.' In fact, I told Jeannine how I felt earlier today and she was hoping with me that you'd bring it up! I knew I couldn't."

"Yes, you could have." He smiled a wry kind-of all knowing smile of assurance.

"But think about it—would you have believed me? Wouldn't you maybe have suspected I was jerking you around? At least you wouldn't have been able to be sure I wasn't jerking you around, right?"

"Well, I guess you have a point Robbi. All I know, is that the day I saw you running down the beach with Vic is the day I knew I'd fallen for you and I've loved you ever since." The memory he was referring to happened at my Mom's birthday lunch after the drunken church boy service, so I'm pretty sure it wasn't the moment I'd fallen for *him*! But all that mattered was that I had now and I knew it. We were holding hands across the table by this point. [...and that's enough from the Peanut Gallery with your accusations of cheesiness. It WAS cheesy and I'm proud of it!]

"I have to ask you Burk: How on earth did you get the courage to ask me this...for lack of a better word...again? How come you weren't scared about being turned down again?"

He shrugged. "Robbi, I knew...know that I love you. I had to ask you about it again. On the plane home from India, I had a lot of time to think about it and I thought, 'Burk are you gonna be a mouse or are you gonna be man?' I chose man." Wow—did you EVER! Okay now he was just plain sexy. I wanted to leave right then and there. We managed to hurry through some appetizers and leave to go back to his place. His roommate, thank goodness, was OUT. And Burk kissed me but he didn't just kiss me—it was a push against-the-wall passionate kiss and he was Ser. i. ous. I put my hand on his chest and pushed him away a little bit and said, "We need to talk...."

"I know I know I know....okay let's talk."

"You know I can't sleep with you unless you marry me, right?"

"Yes I know. You told me that two years ago when we first met. I didn't assume it had changed, but you're not telling me I'm not doing *this*," which was more of the same passionate intentional loving on each other. This went on for oh...I'd say 30 or 40 minutes, even though it was eleven o'clock at night and we both knew I wasn't staying.

But here's the thing: Burk lived in a duplex apartment. His landlord was another single guy from church who lived on the other side of the duplex. He saw Burk's living room light and decided to come over and talk to him about something. As Tom walked up to Burk's front door, he could see us making out through the front window (just so you know, I was...uh...AM... horrifically embarrassed about this up until this moment—not enough I guess, to leave it out of this book, but Egads)! Tom raised his eyebrows and said to himself, "Huh! I guess Burk and Robyn are back together..." Yes Tom, yes we are!

He told Burk about it the next day and we had a good laugh about it, but the thought of him seeing Burk running his hand passionately up and down my side while kissing me still makes me squirm. Even so, I am able to shrug my shoulders a little on this memory because it was eleven o'clock at night!

So the next day, I called Jeannine and told her everything that had happened with Burk on the date and to please keep the news between us for now and she was more than delighted and agreed to keep our relationship on the down-low. She told Cole too which I said was fine, but that was really all who knew for awhile. We just wanted a little privacy to get our sea legs. We didn't want to announce to everyone at church and then be the center of attention. I did tell my Mom, but I was a cool customer about that one. I didn't want it to take her by surprise if it got serious fast, but I didn't want to expose the same squealing like Jeannine and I had shared. I said, "Hey Mom—remember Burk from church? Yeh well...he and I are kind of dating. 'Not sure where it's goin' but just thought I'd tell ya I'm hangin' out with him again." My Mom was great about it and silently I think she was terribly relieved it wasn't another, "I'm back with the Lug" announcement.

Twenty-one:
Re-Initiation and Undoing

The beginning of my courtship with Burk was a bit of an "initiation." Or should I say the beginning of my second courtship with Burk? ...This second way of putting it sorta diminishes the extraordinary nature of it though, because after all I'd been through, before and after our first go around, in addition to all he'd been through over me, we wouldn't have made a decision to play for keeps if neither of us were serious. I was this time. He was this time. Yet because of the history, we had a little explaining to do because he had said some not-so-very-nice things about me to a few of his friends, while meanwhile I had gone around telling people I wasn't attracted to him. Remember Cate's indirect prophecy? I was so close to Cate, I knew she wouldn't say "I told you so" or anything. In fact, I knew she would be thrilled for Burk and me! But the mere fact that she'd predicted it made me think about the several [and, I mean *several*] friends and relatives I'd announced it to, that redheads weren't my type. Never say never. You know how I dislike chichés by now, but I mean this one Sisters: "Never say never!"

I couldn't imagine NOT being attracted to redheads now and in fact, Jeannine and I had spotted the actor Eric Stoltz in the movie *Memphis Belle* and decided Burk looked like a movie star. Jeannine was very good at finding look-alike movie actor/actresses for everyone, and Eric Stoltz was definitely Burk's.

So anyway, I had a few people to profess that to, that I'd changed my mind about Burk being my type. Burk had a tougher task ahead of him than I did though, which was explaining the idea of me to *his* *contingency*. See, he'd been a lot angrier with me over our break up, particularly the way I'd handled the timing of it right before Christmas. He confessed a few days after our get-back-together-Leap-Year date, that maybe...just maybe he might have referred to me as...a...well ..."Bitch" to one or maybe even two people! These happened to be some of his best friends, sooooo Burk had some digging out to do.

At work, Burk had a really good friend who also happened to be his professional mentor: her name was Christina Monchaf. She was already a partner when he was hired in as a first-year associate and assigned to her mentorship. She was a crackerjack! She was an excellent litigator, but also because she was a couple of years older than Burk, she became a confidant as well. Firm law is a big deal for a guy who has clerked for a judge for one year, worked for the prosecutor's office in Saginaw as a public defender, and worked one other year at a small law office prior to moving to Grand Rapids. It was a lot of pressure. One day Christina, after noticing Burk down in the dumps for several days on end, stopped by his office and leaned on the the door frame. "Hey Burk—you don't seem like yourself. Can you stop by and see me later?" Burk looked up from his laptop and the legal brief he'd been writing, and nodded a beleaguered "sure."

Later on, when he went down to her office, she said, "Shut the door." So, I've come to learn that in a law firm, at least in those early days of Burk's career, when a senior partner says, "shut the door," it usually means something unpleasant was about to be verbally shared with you. Burk came in with that feeling of "Oh no...whhhaaaat now?! What did I screw up?!" But Christina didn't say anything about Burk's work product. She looked at him from across her heavy cherry desk and mentioned again, that he didn't seem like himself and she wondered what was up. It was compassion, not complaint. Burk responded, "Why? Is my work suffering? Have I messed up something?"

"No Burk! I'm seriously just concerned about you. What's going on? Did something happen with that girl you were dating?" Burk looked down. It was a week after I'd dumped him to go back to the Lug, back in late 1997. This was the first week of January of 1998.

"Yeh, she dumped me. She went back to her old boyfriend..."

Christina stood straight up in her black Prada pencil skirt and Jimmy Choo pumps. Christina was pissed. "That BITCH!" and so from then on, I was known as a Bitch to the few who were close to Burk at work.

Now, keep in my mind I'd never met any of these people, but outside of the friends Burk had at church, they were the only people in town Burk knew at the time because he was still fairly new to the area and worked around the clock. He didn't have a social life. They were his extended, chosen family. I don't blame him for having felt that way at the time—he was entitled to his process and looking back, I probably did come off that way. But imagine, given his family-like relationship with Christina, two years later Burk going back to her to explain that I was no longer a "bitch," but in fact his girlfriend and he was happy about it. Let's just say he definitely got the same speech from Christina that I would have received from my Mom anytime I'd gotten back together with someone who'd hurt me: "I hope you know what you're doing." Christina took it even a step further with Burk: "She better not hurt you again or I'll kick her ass." Later after meeting Christina, it struck me as funny because she was such a classy chick—an artist, classical pianist, a Shakespearian scholar—not exactly someone who strikes you with the mouth of a motorcycle chick. But that just goes to show how protective she was of Burk.

Speaking of being called a "bitch," it was a word used more than once to describe me by more than one group of people throughout my tenure with Burk. For example, this one time, shortly after I started dating Stephano, my new Italian Stallion boyfriend had been out of town one weekend. I was smitten and already hopelessly devoted. It was a Saturday in May, and it was a gorgeous day out on the Lakeshore. The phone rang and it was Burk out of the blue: "Hey, I'm in Grand Haven down on the boardwalk and I wondered if you wanted to go for a walk to the pier and back, or roller blading or something..." I guess he'd heard I'd broken things off with the Lug for good. Still, I'd been caught off guard and didn't want to hurt his feelings, so I said I was "busy" and couldn't do it today, but "thanks for calling." Now what I SHOULD have said was, "Thanks, Burk, for the invite, but I'm actually seeing someone right now." Why couldn't I just tell the truth?

Here's why I should have admitted that instead of saying I was "busy." Right before Burk called, I was planning to go for a run down to the boardwalk myself, from my house all the way to the pier and back. So I went for my run anyway, reasoning that since it was a Saturday in May, the place would be swamped as it usually is and the chances of seeing him were 'nil. It wasn't swamped, however. Thirty minutes later, I went running towards the pier and Burk came roller blading by me back the other direction. Busted.

That night, Burk called his buddy Decker, remember the one who had come looking for me in the first place and showed up at my door? Well, they were still best buds, and Burk called him and said, "That Bitch! I am sooooooo done with her!" Ahhhhh yes.

Yet another time, I was out at the Kirby Grill, the bar/grill where Burk and I had first met, on a Saturday night for dinner with a girlfriend. We were in the restaurant section of the establishment, in the back. On the way out, we passed by the bar and there sat Burk with Decker. I walked up and said, "Hi" with a big smile. I was just assuming it was okay to be friendly [and was clearly unaware of the way he'd felt altogether about me]. Deck said, "Hi." Burk did not. In fact, Burk stared into his beer then flashed a little side glance that said, "Really? You're saying, 'hi' to me? After all you've done?" Rutrow! I could tell he was ticked off at me still.

"Ohhhhhhkaaaaaaay then. We'll be going." After I left, I found out later as soon as I walked away, he muttered in a low tone, "bitch!", in unison, along with Decker.

So it had been safely established that I was a "bitch" to many of Burk's confidants and he had some work to do in order to "unbitch" me. Decker took it well though and said, "Well okay, Rusty, I hope you know what you're doing, but I'll give her a chance if that's what you want." The next weekend we got together with Deck and his girlfriend Paisley. Now Paisley was a tough cookie and was as smart as a whip. She was from Mississippi and in fact, when she got mad at Decker, his name became a three syllable word: Day-eck-cher. So after being around Paisley a few times and hearing her call Decker Day-eck-err enough, I didn't think I had anything to worry about if someone on that side of Burk's acquaintances thought I was bitchy. Paisley was bossy in a lovely southern way, proud of it and pleased to be identified as such. My concerns melted away pretty fast.

They melted away with Christina too and it turns out that she and I had more in common than even she and Burk had, and it wasn't long before Christina and I were better friends because of it. My friends however (except Jeannine and Cole), were a little more unsure. Please understand. There had been so many men I'd sworn I was crazy about before and here was one I'd actually claimed the opposite. They had a right to assume that it was suspect. So, most of them did have a "we'll see" attitude, but I didn't care. I didn't need their approval—Burk was a class act and a cute one at that. I had him. It was enough.

Our courtship was full of hikes out at Saugatuck State Park, quiet dinners at 'Til Midnight, sharing in ministry together at church, watching sports—especially the Redwings, and also right after we had gotten back together, March Madness was in mad-March full-swing.

The Michigan State Spartans under coach Tom Izzo had a fighting chance. So, every other night for 3 weeks we hung on every basket until State won the NCAA championship that year. We fell in love to MSU basketball. We played frisbee on the beach and in the yard across the street from my house where there was a vacant lot. We walked to beachfront decks and had drinks while the sun went down. It was romantic and fun, and we tried to really enjoy the time, assuming at some point we'd get engaged.

After five and a half months though, I began to get antsy. I was thirty-four, Burk was three years younger than me. I know men don't go around thinking about time the way women do even when they are completely serious about the person they are dating. They don't think about it much because they don't really have to. Their sperm works longer than our eggs. So the antsy-ness was fair on my side, but it was also understandable that Burk wasn't feeling the heat to the degree that I was.

Twenty-two:
Calma Calma Down Doobeedo Down Down

Burk was not a direct communicator. I don't like trying to figure how a person might be feeling based on a collection of recent data clues. I like it when people just speak directly to their point. Out loud. It's just easier then mental telepathy if you know what I mean. If there was one attribute I didn't like about Burk, this was it. He wasn't bad at it all of the time—just much of the time! It's not surprising though, because it seems as though he got this lovely quality from his mother, who for the record, was the best facial-expression communicator in the entire world. One raise of the eyebrow produced "I'm sorry" from anyone in the room. One glance downward and everyone knew she "disapproved." But the big lip is perhaps the one she was best at: like a five-year-old, she could get people to come running to her rescue (whatever the rescue-du-jour might be), without saying a word. Oh and then there were the tears—the silent crying: tears streaming down her face followed by a gentle dab of the Kleenex. It absolutely leveled any man, woman, or child that came across her path, except for...you guessed it! Me.

Like I said, I prefer that people talk out loud when they want something instead of making you guess and then being mad at you if you guess wrong.

Lahteedah. It is what it is and it was what it was. Viv was a lovely creature in many respects [like, she made the best oatmeal bread on the planet and she'd baby you if you were sick, like making chicken soup from scratch]. But Burk had learned a few bad habits from the master. So, you know my track record with the lack of commitment from the past slitherers and slatherers in my life? Given that, I didn't have a large capacity for being treated like a wife if I wasn't a wife.

For example, Burk wanted to buy a Suburban and he refused to buy it unless I was comfortable driving it. In the past, I would have made an assumption that this meant an engagement ring was coming soon, yet I had been wrong with this type of deduction with the Lug— even after we were engaged twice and looked at several houses together let alone vehicles, but I knew that the accumulation of things, albeit a car or a house, or a lawnmower or a sailboat, or even a dog meant I might be getting married, but then again? I might not be. Stephano did this to me too: he talked about marriage right out of the box, which is one of the reasons I embraced his family to the degree that I did, which is one of the reasons the break up had been devastating. I'd heard this, "you're gonna be my wife" line several times before.

Now I know in Burk's case he was really trying to be inclusive. But I couldn't play husband and wife. Oh....Yeh...SURE you want to get married?! I'll believe it when I see it! It wasn't Burk's fault. It was the fault of my past wounds of course, but it was very real. There had been a lot of this going on too, because Burk had taken me out to visit his parents in Massachusetts the month prior. Whenever you get on a plane to go spend time with a serious boyfriend's family, it's a statement! If they live across town? Not so much. When air travel is involved? It's a big deal. I told Burk I preferred to get on a plane as an engaged woman if we were to go out to his parent's. He talked me out of the engagement part, assuring me of his sincerity in long talk after a long talk, with allusions to secret plans. So, between the purchasing of his new car...and also the trip to Massachusetts to stay with his folks...and *also* not to mention Burk spending every waking moment with me when he wasn't working, made me believe he wanted to get married; but, it also made me wonder why he was stalling on getting engaged, and it was beginning to scare me a little.

One Sunday afternoon there was a knock on my front door. It was Burk. There he was, without calling. He lived 35 minutes away. We usually didn't hang out on Sunday evenings because I had Monday morning classes and field assignments to prepare for. Burk too, used Sunday nights to get himself back into work mode. So it was a surprise to see him standing on my front porch.

"Hi Babe, What's going on??" And that was the beginning of a long dissertation of bad bad very-bad, no good communication. He walked in, shaking his head and looking down at his Converse, tennis-shoed feet, acting frustrated and nervous. Whining, he responded speaking very quickly,

"Well, I opened the mail after you left today and I got this mission trip support letter from Sheila and she wrote a note at the bottom and the note said, 'Rumor has it you're an engaged man!' And I didn't like it. I'm tired of everyone pressuring me and telling me and—"

"Burk, you can't honestly be serious that you expect me to stand here and listen to you spewing that to. My. Face???" He looked perplexed like he didn't realize he was being completely inappropriate until I pointed it out. I continued, "You're seriously standing here complaining at the prospect of being engaged? To *me*? About *me*? You're acting like she's accusing you of being engaged to Morticia Adams?! After you took me to Massachusetts to stay with your family? Had me drive your new car around and are constantly seen with me everywhere? You don't think others are assuming that you are serious about me? For goodness sake Burk: I'm 34. You're 31. Are you unaware of what is going on in your own life??" I was almost shrieking now. I was hopping up and down on the balls of my feet. I was pointing at him.

He continued whining still: "I just don't like other people telling me that I'm supposed to get married." I remained utterly quiet, which you've probably noticed is not my usual modus operandi. Then I quietly and calmly found these words coming of out of my mouth that even I was surprised to hear:

"Then don't get married Burk. In FACT, stop treating me like a wife since I'm not a wife. IN *FACT*, I do not want to see you again until you are ready to get engaged. I'm done." I meant it too. I was walking him back to the front door now. And that was that: I'd offered the ultimatum of the century. He was in my house a total of 240 seconds. Five minutes ago I had a fantastic boyfriend I was probably marrying, yet without any warning, he stops by whining to me, about being accused of wanting to marry me, and boom, he's out of my life.

Do I need to explain more about why I didn't think Burk was very good at direct communication? Nope, I didn't think so.

He was stunned: "Rob! You don't mean that!"

"I absolutely mean it, Burk. Out you go. I'll talk to you when you're ready to get married. And I mean REH. DEE. Don't call me. Don't come over unless you want to get married and you're willing to do it that second!"

Now, I didn't really mean I wouldn't have an engagement and a wedding. But I didn't want him pulling the Lug's shit on me, as in: Here's the ring and this will let you know I'm thinking about being committed to you," which was never said out loud but was ultimately true, TWICE. So, I wanted Burk to think that if he came back, he better be prepared to run right over to the Justice of the Peace.

So, out he did in fact go. He was mystified and acting befuddled as if to say, "Wow—this wasn't the outcome I expected from coming over here. What have I done? How did this happen?" I looked out the window and watched him run his fingers through his hair climbing up into the new Suburban. Once he got in, he just sat there for a sec staring into the space straight ahead of him before he reluctantly pulled out of the parallel parking spot across the tiny street from my house.

Now: in Burk's defense, we had only been dating for six months but it was a serious six months. EVERYONE thought we were getting married (not true with the Lug or Stephano. In fact, there were many in both scenarios hoping against it, such as Cole and company.) Not only did everyone think Burk and I were getting married, everyone was *hoping* we were getting married. And why do you suppose Burky-Poo that everyone thinks we're getting married? Because you've let everyone *think it* by the way you have conducted yourself over the past six months like YOU WANT TO GET MARRIED TO ME! For the love of Mike! [sidebar: who is Mike and why do we love him? Just askin'.]

Jeeyimity. It exhausts me just writing the reliving of this scene.

Twenty-three: When Pigs Fly

I thought Burk would cave in a day. I imagined him getting home Sunday night even and already calling me! Nope. Everything was quiet. By the next night when I had heard nothing from him, I thought I saw some tumbleweed roll through the living room as I walked by. It had only been a little over 24 hours though. "He's probably teaching me a lesson," I reasoned.

But by Tuesday night and still nothing?? I was getting scared and weepy. Maybe he's not coming back. Should I call him? Do I need this silly break up? Should I give him a chance to warm up his feet? I thought this through for a bit: I lifted the laptop off my cross-legged position, stretched out my legs and crossed them at the ankle on the coffee table. I stared into space out of my own window, which is not something I did too often because the houses in town were separated by the width of a single driveway. There were no garages to buffer the view. Sometimes staring off into space accidentally produced some unfortunate information from earthling neighbors. This time I was lucky though, since no one next door seemed to be home, but from my overstuffed chair, I could see into their living room and to the little yellow pillow sandwiched between the arm rest and the remote control on their sofa.

I zoomed out and let the pillow get fuzzy because I needed to weigh some options. Is this about loneliness versus companionship only? 'Cause if it is, I'm picking up the phone. I LOVED Burk. I didn't want to live my life without him in it. But if it's about all the elements of life I've said I've always wanted, such as marriage, having babies, and raising kids along with a Good Knight, then I had to hold off. Getting back with him for companionship only wouldn't achieve the end game I'd prayed for. Burk wasn't in a hurry and at 31; he didn't have to be in a hurry. Men don't have biological clocks like women do—they can father healthy children until their equipment breaks off. We gals have a window and every year we get older the risks go up for our bodies and our babies.

So let's say Burk was definitely planning on popping the question in a couple of years. Well, if he was going to marry me anyway and if he was hoping to have children with *me* anyway? It behooved him to step on it because of the closing window. So I arrived back to this spot on the circle of my analysis, not before I went around a few more times mind you, but I settled back at the same point: assuming it's me he wants and my babies, now is better than later. Therefore, I need to let him feel the loss right now, even if I have to feel it too. Good. I have a plan in place. Whew.

By the NEXT night however, I was borderline hysterical. I called up Jeannine (I hadn't told my family yet because I didn't want to worry them if it turned out to be just a little spat...) but I couldn't take it anymore. "Oh my gosh Robbi, he ADORES you. He's not going anywhere!! He's not going anywhere!" admonishing my concerns.

"But he doesn't like feeling like everyone is deciding for him."

"That's ridiculous. No one is doing that. It's because he's already decided. He just can't push himself to pull the trigger on a decision he's already friggin' made." Well, and Jeannine was right because although I didn't know it at the time, Burk had gone to see Pastor Finn who was a really great dude. Pastor Finn had been firefighter in Chicago for twenty years before going into ministry work. Pastor Finn had seen some crap, if you know what I mean. He was the real deal.

Burk sat down in his office at the church. Burked whined [what is it with the whining? How could my very Good Knight be a whiner??? I'm just sayin', it doesn't match the rest of his otherwise charming image...]. He whined some more, basically telling the same weepy story to Pastor Finn that he'd already said to me [Please hear whiny-valley girl voice]: I'm Tyyy-high-errrdd Pastor Feeeeeeiiiiiinn. Why is everybodddddddy making me get ennnnnngaheeeeeyyyyged?" Finn said nothing. He looked right at Burk and then looked down and opened his drawer. He dug around in there until he was able to reach something out of the far back of the drawer. As he lifted it out, Burk thought he saw something that looked like a Groucho Marx big nose/glasses set. He kind of did except...the nose part that sits above the black mustache right underneath the big round glasses was not actually a nose. It was a big penis instead! Finn put the glasses on and looked right at Burk.

"You are being a Dicknose. Marry that girl!" and with that, he took the gasses off and shoved them into the back of his drawer.

"Thaaaaat's it?" Burk asked, seemingly shocked that Finn was finished giving him advice. Burk had been hoping for a little more pastoral direction.

"That's it Dude." Burk sat there for a minute to see if Finn-the-Pastor may have a sarcastic word or joke to go along with it because he was usually hilarious. Not this time. He just flashed Burk a knowing grin and pointed to the door. Burk walked out the door muttering something about driving all the way over here and taking time out of his day for this crap and that's just great, Finn—I came to get an encouraging word from my pastor and really? That's it? Blah blah blah and all that. So although I didn't find out about this until much later,

Jeannine was right that Burk had already decided. Pastor Finn knew it too, which is why he put on the dicknose and told Burk he was being stupid. It was the reassurance of a few, that ultimately kept me from panicking too much.

I did feel this unlikely peace at times. I heard a voice that said, "You're not supposed to feel peace. You broke up with your boyfriend. You're an Idiot." But I pushed them away. I knew who Burk was. I knew he loved me. So I vacillated from worried to peaceful and from weepy back to peaceful and then from sick-to-my-stomach with a side of peace. Have you ever felt sick to your stomach with a side of peace? It felt icky but I somehow suspected that the icky wasn't going to be permanent. I was trying to embrace my change in attitude about my life and the Hope sign over my toilet, that regardless of marriage or having babies, I was worthwhile; that my life had worth either way...

By Thursday I was riding the peace wave—nervous, but hopeful. I hadn't gone four days without seeing or speaking with Burk in six months. I was trying to go through my life as normally as I could; I was still working out and going to classes, singing the anthem, running my Dad to appointments, and going to music practice. That night the phone rang and it was Burk. I was so relieved to hear his voice, but I was playing it cool! "Hi Burk."

"Hi Robbi. How are you???" We were best friends after all. I could tell he missed me as a friend at least even if nothing else, because he was so sincere.

"Well, to be honest, it's been kind of a weird week—"

"TELL me about it!" Now we were simpatico—I could feel that neither of was making stuff up or trying to sound a certain way. [Hey Burk: I am liking this direct communication.]

"Whatcha up to? You sound like you're driving?"

"Yeh, I am. I'm on the way home from Grand Rapids. I had dinner with some friends from work..."

"Bill and Christina, Rick, Jeff etc?"

"Yeh—same old crowd. You weren't there, so...I missed you though..." Now I was huddled up in a ball on my bedroom floor like a little kid with my own arms wrapped around myself for comfort and as if the receiver on the phone *was* Burk, I clutched it as close to myself as I could. I asked him,

"Did you tell them we were apart??"

"Well, I told them you were busy. You know I didn't want to talk about how much I was missing you." There it was! 'HUGE release of breath from my chest as I was trying to keep it silent on the phone. I was pretty sure he might be coming back around but then again I was also pretty sure he wasn't; having him directly communicate that he was missing me produced an inordinate amount of reassurance. So I had to ask:

"So...whatcha thinkin'?" ...and it just hung there in the silence for what seemed as long as a class lecture from Charlie Brown's teacher.

Finally, "I'm thinking about a lot of things, Robbi. You were right that I wasn't being fair to you." Suddenly, cool was over. I was finished with cool. I got anxious and wanted to tell him, "Drive over here this minute!"—I refrained but I needed to know what was happening with him and the topic of him in my life. I loved him too much.

"Burk! What is going on? What are we doing? What are you doing?!" I know I sounded desperate.

"Hang tight, Robbi. I love you. I will be in touch with you soon." And as much as it pained me, I knew I had to say it,

"Okay, but you know what I said about calling me or coming over or us being together unless you were ready...I meant what I said Burk." I was almost crying now.

"I know" he said comfortingly. "I know, Baby. Hang tight. I will hang tight too." I hung up. I was balling. This sucked.

Fridays were light class days for me so I went to class and took the rest of the day off from homework. I decided I needed a distraction. I threw myself into my house trying not to think about the fact that I had spent the past twenty-four Friday nights with Burk. I cleaned, I went out and rented a movie, I got a pizza and a bottle of wine. I celebrated all of the things I remembered I had that were good, back from when I'd had that epiphany a couple years before: good family, baby niece, cute house, new career which I'm damn good at thank-you-very-much, and great friends. I refused to feel sorry for myself but just dove in and swam around in thankful—I did not leave the sea of thankful for the rest of the evening or even the next morning. I planned my day for Saturday so I wouldn't have "dead time," starting with a run and then plotted a trip to TJ Maax where I did eventually end up. I invested in some retail therapy procuring, three new pairs of shoes! I spoke to Jeannine earlier and she'd invited me over to hangout later on and see my niece and watch a movie over there. I had *plans*. I was not sitting by the phone.

So, I raced in the house from TJ Maxx with my bag of shoes spilling forth and when one fell out of the bag in my front hallway and I almost tripped over it, I realized I was racing around after too many Diet Cokes and subsequent adrenaline rushes. I took a deep breath. "Wow," I thought: "If he calls my bluff and really doesn't want to get married, then I am going to have to get comfortable with being alone again. I'm going to have to slow down. I can't continue to go at this speed...I could break an ankle on a new shoe and who does that help?" No one.

I took my own advice. I took a deep breath—in through the nose—out through the mouth.

Whew.

Okay.

Now what? (I think I heard crickets for a sec.)

I knocked around the house until the time came to leave for Jeannine and Cole's. But then my phone rang.

Da da dah dummmmmmnnn. It was Burk. I almost didn't answer it. I didn't like that I seemed to be there every time he called. I wanted to be obtuse. But then I remembered that I'd given up on those games several years ago. Trying to re-accept my grownup self, I answered.

"Hey,"...making it look deliberate as in, I know it's you Burk and I'm choosing to answer the phone—I may not next time. Just sayin'.

"Hey back! What are you doing right now?"

"Uhhh...well..I was just getting ready to go to Jeannine and Cole's..."

"Oh...well...I'm in town and I was wondering if I could stop by."

"Well...Burk the thing is..."

"Robbi, I know the 'thing.' I need to talk to you. I was hoping you would go for a walk with me—" his voice trailing off slightly...

I exhaled a tight breath that I'm pretty sure he heard and said, "Okay. I'll hang."

I waited. I didn't even run to the bathroom to look in the mirror. I had no idea how I looked. I didn't care. I knew this was the moment I either got engaged or got on with my own life by myself. It was a throw-down moment. But, I was willing to keep the jury out until I'd heard the testimony.

When he got there, I was inwardly chomping at the bit but trying very hard to appear calm and collected; I opened the front door and stayed in motion swinging it open and then turning my back and kept walking to grab my keys off the counter. I didn't want to make eye contact. I was kind to him of course, but was trying to be cool....like this were any day—or any walk—or any person—any moment.

We walked down the street in a gingerly manner. It was weird to be this close to him and not touch him. Now here's what's funny about this: Burk had envisioned going for a walk to the beach, except that he never said out loud we were going for a walk to the beach [because I'm telepathic 'doncha know...all indirect communicators assume this about the person they're indirectly communicating with.] The beach was a good mile or so away and it was up and down hilly streets to get there, so it took a good 30-40 minutes. Burk had planned it in his head to take about five minutes. He did not tell me this. I assumed we were going for a walk around the block so I didn't wear tennis shoes, I wore cheap flip flops because that's what I had on when he got there. So, what Burk had thought would be this lovely little romantic stroll, became a tedious long and sweaty excursion that was killing my feet! I didn't complain out loud but it became obvious that the idea in his head wasn't matching reality, because there were these huge gaping holes of silence along the way, in addition to the wincing facial expressions pouring off of me, given my ouchy feet.

He desperately tried to fill the holes with small talk which of course was absurd given my six-day-old ultimatum that I did not want to see him again, unless he were to propose. Then if that weren't bad enough, it started to rain. It was just sprinkling but again, not what Burk had envisioned when he planned it.

After an eternity we finally arrived at the beach. Now, if you're a hopeless romantic like me and watched enough princess movies, sappy romantic comedies, and episodes of *The Bachelor*, then perhaps you're expecting that we came upon a scene of beach—blanketed canopies and lit candles with wine chilling. Or perhaps you're expecting that Burk would scoop me up, twirl me around in a circle and declare his undying love for me. Or at the very least, for the man to drop to his knees for crying out loud and look up at me with puppy dog eyes and ask me to be his wife while placing a ring on my finger. Okay...ummm....so please lower your expectations!

Like I said, we arrived at the beach in the rain and I had a blister forming on the ball of my left foot. Burk wasn't even holding my hand at this point, but seemed to be scanning the beach for the "perfect spot." Since it was raining, the beach was sparsely populated so there wasn't too much of a chance he could pick an un-private spot. Truly, there was NO one there which was unthinkable for an early fall weekend in our beach town. Finally, he stopped, sat down and motioned for me to sit beside him. He looked out at the lake where the line meets the sky. He said, "I have something for you."

He took a piece of paper out of his pocket and handed it to me. He had written me a letter.

To be honest, I'm not even exactly sure what it said except that he loved me, he wanted to marry me and that writing it to me was the best way he knew how to express it. He admitted that sometimes when he tried to say things it just never came out right [I'll say!...given his whining about Sheila's postscript!]

So although, I wouldn't suggest it was the most romantic proposal on record, it was the most sincere. Minus the pomp and circumstance, I actually believed him, which was important after what I'd been through with men and promises of years gone by. I needed to believe him and I did. After thoughtfully finishing his letter, I looked at him sitting next to me in the sand and with a wry smile said, "Yes Burk. I will marry you."

And before I could kiss him he said nervously with a note of apology in his tone, "Now...umm...I didn't buy a ring for you because I wanted us to go this week and pick it out together but for the meantime, I have my grandma's ring and I was wondering if you wear it until we can get you yours??" And ya know what? I realized that this was absolutely what I loved about Burk, that he didn't put a piece of jewelry before a commitment to me and that he was willing to explain to others that the commitment was about marriage and forever, not the value of a "thing," and that our life together was more important than the trimmings.

Don't get me wrong—I wanted a pretty ring but not more than lifelong commitment. I wanted a beautiful wedding but not more than a beautiful life. A wedding was one day. A marriage is a lifetime. So, even though I'd put my time in by any gal's standards and was therefore deserving of a fancy proposal, engagement and wedding with all of the trimmings, more than anything it made sense to me now, that after *all* of it, it was just him. And me. None of it mattered. I had a letter, a sweet little family heirloom around my finger and the promise of a devoted man who would stay that way. It was MORE than enough.

So, on the walk home we laughed so hard about how awkward the walk to the beach had been. "Is your foot okay??"

"Nah," I said, "but I don't care!" We were both a little frustrated that Burk couldn't get a cell signal that close to the lake because we wanted to call everybody! But looking back, I'm glad we had that time. What was of annoyance on the trip there, was time to treasure on the way back.

"Hey, who else knows about this Burk? Do my parents know?"

"Yeh. I went to see them first before calling you. I asked your Dad if I could marry you and he said 'Oh Boy' like he always does and your Mom is flipping out!"

"Okay, so my parents know. Do YOUR parents know???"

"Robbi, no else but your parents know...and ...uh...well I think Pastor Finn is maybe suspecting. I went to see him the other day. We had a talk..."

"A talk?"

"Yeh, I'll tell you about it later...after a drink!" And with that we ran home. Burk was carrying my flip flops and I was darting on and off to the sidewalk to make the most out of the cushioned grass. And guess what? The moment we turned onto my street it stopped raining! Oh well—it was still the best day of my life up until that point! We ran in and called Jeannine first: Before she could finish the "lo" of "Hel-lo," I interrupted and spewed, "Guesswhat guesswhatguesswhat guesswhat guesswhat?????!!!!!"

"Oh my GOSH, WHAT??!!"

"I'm engaged! Burk and I are getting married!!" She started crying.

"Robbi??! Oh my gosh—I am so happy and then with her hand muffling the receiver, I heard her yell, "Cole, you're sister is getting married!" He shouted back and also muffled, "To who this time?!" Always the smart ass—he couldn't help him himself. Laughing at his own joke, he picked up the phone and said, "Just kidding Just kidding. It better be Burk and I better be invited!"

"Yeh yeh. Wanna talk to your new family member?"

"Yeh! Put him on!" So they chatted, Cole congratulating Burk and Burk receiving the congratulations and telling Cole he was excited and it was privilege to be become a part of our family. I stood there bouncing up and down on my heels whispering, "Hey...let me talk to Jeannine again before you hang up..." then in a louder whisper so I made sure he knew not to hang up, "Don't forget—I need to talk to Jeannine again." He gave me this look where his eyebrows went up and eyes bugged out at me, "For goodness freakin' sake, Woman!?" He finally handed the phone back to me, and I said,

"Jeannine—we don't even have a date yet, but whenever it is, will you be my matron of honor?" I could hear baby Talia cooing in the background.

"Seriously??? You're asking me right now? You already know you're picking me?!!"

"Of course, Silly!"

"Well, Yes yes, YES, I will be your matron of honor. But 'oh no,' I have this short spiky hair—I can't be your matron of honor with short spiky hair???!! Do I have time to grow it out or are you doing this next week??" She was seriously concerned about her hair. Here's why: Jeannine was a an experimenter of changing hairstyles. When I met her, she was a long dark-sandy blonde. Then when she married Cole, her hair was California-girl blonde. Then at some point, she got it cut to the shoulder and went red [it was Woody Woodpecker red until she went in and the professional stylist fixed it to acceptable red...] Then, she dyed it back blonde close to her natural color again a year or so later. That's what it was when Talia was born.

However, within a month of Talia's little baby life, she had become a very strong-fisted little baby and liked to yank on Jeannine's locks during feedings and poor Jeannine: after pre-term labor, Magnesium Sulfate, steroids, moon face, weighing more than Cole the day before Talia was born [yes, I had permission to include that] AND having her nether region "checked" by countless doctors, nurses, techs, medical students, and at one point we even think the Coke machine guy in the hospital might have grabbed a gander while she was in labor because there were so many people in and out of her room, given the delicate nature of her entire pregnancy. Jeannine was done with the physically painful sacrifices she would make for baby Talia. After all Jeannine had been through, having her hair pulled was the final straw and it's where she drew the line and declared her suffering finis'. So, she went and got her hair CHOPPED off. Ten inches gone just like that—her hair was an inch long, bleached blonde and she wore it spiky.

She loved it and she wore it well as she did all of her dos. Right now actually, she happens to have long dark brown hair after years of a longer white funky style she also looked great in. Then one day, just like the haircut day, she dyed it chocolate velvet brown like Angelina Jolie. She's been a brunette for awhile now, but we never know. [Sidebar: correction: she was a brunette when I wrote the first draft of my book. She is now red again on this here second draft, but with black on the bottom underlying layer.

—Third Draft: The underlying layer is now purple.

—Fourth Draft: Strawberry blonde and long but with bangs. Really, Jeannine's hair deserves its own chapter...]

My point though: I loved Jeannine for being willing to change her hair for my wedding but I didn't care. I. Did. Not. Care. See, perspective is everything, People—these little things that folks get so upset about, like what their bridesmaids' hairstyles are? I was getting married to a Good Knight! Hairstyle schmairstyle. One of my friends, Lizzy, refused to be a bridesmaid given that she figured out she'd be 8 months pregnant at the time of my wedding. She had just found out she was expecting her first a few weeks prior to my news. Again, big preggo bridesmaid? Didn't care! I actually thought it would be fun to have an eclectic grouping of the wonderful war torn soldier-rettes who had walked with me through this journey of finding my Knight. But Lizzy refused because she was scared she might go into labor or something at the wedding and ruin all of the photographs or the ceremony itself. I finally talked her into doing a scripture reading and after an arduous back and forth, she finally relented.

But back to Jeannine: she was not having the spiky deal. I told her it was up to her and she said I deserved a perfect fairytale princess wedding and she, as my matron of honor refused to stand out in the photographs forever as, "the one who didn't have good judgment." For the love of Mike.

The funny thing is that with all of these ladies worrying about ruining the pictures or the event itself with the way they looked, one family member who shall remain nameless, actually wore a bright red floor length dress, which would have been fine except that the photographer put her in the front row of the family photo: so, there I am in my white dress with champagne accents—there's the bridesmaids in their flowing champagne dresses and all of the men in their black tuxes. And the gal in red, whom you can't help but stare at? Right there in front. Is the focus on me, the bride, in the photograph? [Did I mention I've waited 34 years to get married?!] Nope. The focus is most certainly on her in the photo, which I think is hilarious. But it just goes to show that no matter how hard one tries to make things perfect for a wedding, they never will be. To this day, both Jeannine and Lizzy find this whole photograph outcome just as ironic as I do.

But yes, back to phone calling of our big news: Jeannine and I hung up and she promised to begin looking on line immediately for how to grow her hair into a more becoming and sophisticated style.

And then we called Burk's folks. (We waited to call mine since they already knew it was going down.) After Burk's folks answered the phone and Burk told them, I could hear squealing on the other end. Burk stuck his finger in his ear to try to pop the sound barrier since his ear was plugged. Suffice it to say Burk's parents were overjoyed. When I say "Over"-joyed, I meant it because when Burk handed the phone to me so I could also be congratulated personally, they continued on with the squealing—there was a shrieky nature to it! They never stopped from when Burk handed the phone to me—it was almost like they were singing a song—there were no pauses even when I said "hi." Just continual accolades and overjoyment.

"Oh HIIIIIIIIIIIIIIIIIIIIIII Robyn DEAR!!!!! Oh Robyn Robyn Robyn, YOU are our Daughter-in-LOVE!"

"Daughter-in-love?" *What did you just call me?* I didn't say the second part out loud, but I was definitely distracted by the remark. There's no way to say it—I felt immediately awkward.

"Oh yes, not 'Daughter-in-LAW' for goodness sake!! You're WAY too special for that. You are our daughter-in-LUHHHHHHHHHVE!!!!!!!"

Sidebar: how can someone love me when someone does not yet know me? Hmmmmmm. I'd met and or spoken to them a handful of times. They lived out East, too far away for the frequency that speeds up relationships. They were lovely people but I didn't think I knew them quite well enough for them to drip on and on like this. I'm from a huge family and no one drips about anyone—no one gets dripped on...but anyway, I did the best I could with the accolades and shrieking and dripping "love" that came through the receiver. Burk flashed me a look and mouthed. "I'm sorry—they're just excited..." Yes, well...Clearly they're excited. I was polite and said, only to the degree that I felt honest, that I 'loved' them too and that yes, the planning would be fantastic, and yes, we were probably coming out for Christmas (Christmas??—It's Labor Day: Fall semester classes just started three days ago. I just got engaged. I'm not really thinking about Christmas) and uh-huh, there sure is a lot to do, and no, that I didn't need any help in the short term and no, I did not feel overwhelmed by the undertaking of the wedding while being in school full time [ahhh—perhaps you've forgotten I'm thirty-four and that I've been collecting data on how I want my wedding to be for about fifteen years or so? Have you forgotten that I've had a tad bit of field...experience?] and but of course, if I think of anything I will absolutely let you know. Oh and of course, as soon as we choose a date, we will be sure to let you know that as well—yes I understand you have a lot of family to also inform.

Okay, this daughter-in-love needed to get off the phone now.

My engagement now was 30 minutes old and I looked at Burk and said, "Burk, they called me '*their* Daughter-In-Love.' We're not even married yet. Like...I'm not even a *daughter-in*-LAW yet and they've already fast forwarded me to 'love' on the first date." Burk explained that his mother especially, had won the award for the cheesiest comments mixed with chichés that he'd ever known and it was just their way of wanting me to feel accepted. I ultimately let it go but not before I asked, "What if we'd been in person to tell them. Then what what would they have done??? [i.e. the phone call having been already over-the-top in my humble self-sufficient independent opinion.] He shrugged and said, I don't know but my Dad might have picked you up or something. My mom perhaps would have showered you with kisses. I shuddered at the thought. Ay yi yi. The only person I wanted showering me with kisses was Burk!

Burk's parents certainly came on a little strong, but what I found out later is that Viv is the most social of social creatures! [Let's use the metaphor of "squirrels" for the sake of making this point, shall we? We shall. Ahem....: Viv is the most social of squirrels to have ever shared a nut at a squirrel party.] My point? Despite her appearance, which is Mary Poppins-esque, the woman can make a friend ANYWHERE, including in a Harley bar with a Duck-Dynasty'd-bearded-biker dude, should she happen to be in a Harley Bar, I mean. So yeh, she was a little drippy and would spew one-liner clichés [...and you know how much I LOVE clichés], while Burk's dad, Clark, would ride the coattails of her social talent and would chime in whenever he anticipated a clear opening. I just didn't know it at the time that this came from a good place in them, so it did put me off a little. I didn't have a choice but to dismiss it for now though, because all I could think about was that the man I adored had just asked me to be his wife; call me cray cray, but it has a way of edging itself into the forefront of one's mind, dismissing all other topics of distraction.

That night, we sat on the Snug Harbor deck over looking the Grand Haven Channel and we were both beaming. I looked at him and asked, "So I'm really engaged, right? This is really happening, right? You're not going to get nervous or cold feet or change your mind or—"

"Robbi: it takes me a long time to make decisions, but once I make a decision, I never go back on my word. Of course it's real. Of course it's happening. I was dragging my feet before our engagement, but now that I've decided, I can't marry you fast enough. I'll do it whenever you want—before Christmas if you think we can get it together..."

I believed him. And I had good reason to because he was a Good Knight.

The next week, we decided on the first week of March for a wedding date and so it meant we'd be engaged for six months. From a practical standpoint, if we weren't eloping and were going to have the kind of ceremony we wanted with certain important people in attendance, then we had to have enough time to coordinate it. And besides, Jeannine needed time to grow out her hair!

Twenty-four: Daughter-In-Dislike

Right before Thanksgiving my sweet Daddy fell and broke his hip. He had been in failing health for awhile, on a slow steady decline for ten long years. The slow steady decline of constant illness became our "new normal" to the degree that I kind of quit waiting for the "other shoe to drop." My family was so used to his health challenges and extraordinary bounce-backs, that it caught us by surprise that the doctors began to suggest he may not come back from this injury.

He was in the hospital for two weeks and did have surgery, so of course and as usual, we expected him to heal up and come home. But he ended up having to go to nursing care this time after the hospital released him. For the first time in his life, he wasn't going to be home for Christmas. It sounds dramatic, I know, that he wasn't "home for Christmas" like a deployed soldier, when he was actually just across town in nursing care. But still, my Mom wasn't having it and pulled some strings against doctor's, nurse's and the committee of "they's" orders, and worked it out to have him actually spend the day of Christmas at home. For once in her life, I guess she managed to be politically correct in her use of careful language.

The problem was, I'd already committed to fly to Massachusetts for Christmas with Burk's family before my Dad's accident. I was overtly torn between the joy of experiencing an important holiday with Burk's family, my new extended family, and the traditions of old. It didn't sit right in my spirit given my Dad's recent injury. My Mom gave me her blessing though, which helped. I mean, a grown adult can't sit around waiting for their parents' approval in and with every decision because it's unachievable! They're not always going to approve or agree, so I had to do what I felt was right on the season's eve of getting married. But in this circumstance, I was grateful to have it. "Go Rob," she'd said. "You've always been there for your Dad. He knows you love him!" So I went. But not before Burk and I went to the nursing home to have a special Christmas with him; we were going there almost everyday throughout December anyway. I'm not sure if he really absorbed the experience or not though. I felt like he was unaware but his doctors said to treat him the same as always because maybe he was "with" us, but just couldn't express it.

But out in North Dighton, Massachusetts, Burk's parents welcomed us with Christmas cheer. We flew out on a snowy, December twenty-third morning. I had so many expectations of what it meant to spend Christmas with my fiancé. Our wedding was just nine weeks after Christmas, so this was a big deal. Their home, although I'd been before, was adorable: it was a Colonial with a single candle in each of the eight front windows, a stoked up wood burning stove, and when we walked in, it smelled like homemade bread. Between the flight out of Grand Rapids and our connection in Detroit, I'd managed to ignite some Christmas excitement in my heart despite the yearnings for my Dad's health. As soon as we walked in, Clark asked, "Would you like a glass of wine?" It was high noon. I was thaaarilled!

"Of course I'll have some, thanks!" But the dynamic of Christmas there was soooooo different than what I was used to. Burk was an only child, both sides of his parents' extended families were spread all over the U.S., so it was just the four of us. I was used to people people people and it was so quiet quiet quiet. It was quaint and had all the trappings of Christmas; Viv had a Father Christmas doll collection. There were stockings stuffed (and I'm not kidding: they were hand knit by Viv and so once they were stuffed, they stretched out two feet long and looked like the shape of Indiana). There were cute little metal, hand-painted children's toys from Clark's childhood that lined the stairs, and there was prime rib roast for Christmas dinner. I laid awake in my own room across the hall from Burk staring at the ceiling thinking about how the next time we stayed here, Burk and I would be in the same bed and how at thirty-five years of age, I was really getting married. It seemed surreal or unreal but I was so content inside about Burk and our future together. Being here in Massachusetts with Burk's little family had made me take an unintended step away from life so I could see with some perspective. Gosh it was so busy all of the time— full time school, three part-time jobs, planning a wedding, student teaching next semester and of course my Dad's health was now in question in an even bigger way than it had been in the past. Being out of West Michigan had given me an unexpected pause.

I surmised I wouldn't have been as contemplative had Burk had a big hustling bustling family like mine at the holidays; if so, I would have flitted from one thing to the next as Christmas typically dictates given calendar obligations, shopping and the preparing. But once I got here, the work was all done on my end. I had nothing to do except ask Viv if she wanted help with anything, which she refused. I've come to learn in my life that hostesses do this: hostesses feel that it will put upon their guests if they don't do absolutely everything themselves, and especially in Viv's case during this particular year, because she wanted to make it a perfect Christmas for me and didn't want me to be bogged down with "work." Still, it felt weird to sit still.

And that's how I started thinking about what came next. That's why I had time to analyze the situation and that's why...well...I kind of pushed the envelope on a teensy weensy little topic of frustration that came to light with Burk. So, during the day of December twenty-six, we had gone on a day trip to the Vanderbilt Mansion at The Breakers in Providence, Rhode Island. (Going to Clark and Viv's was cool because they lived a two-hour drive from anything and everything. You could see any sight of interest with a day trip, including Boston, Cape Cod, Newport, Rhode Island, and Concorde, (Pennsylvania). I was a little tired:—the travel, the emotional joy of getting married mixed with the uncertainty of my own family, and being away from my Dad while he was in a nursing "home," and also the normal let down one feels after Christmas day given the rush and excitement that proceeds it. Once we'd been there a solid three days, I'd begun to notice that Burk wasn't really himself around me with his parents. You see, the three of them were very tight because Clark was a career military officer, and since he and Viv had only one child and the three of them moved together every eighteen months and all over the world, the perforation of their "gig" was very difficult.

When I combined their tight bond with the fact that I was away from my own family and my Dad was especially ill, even for him, along with the fact that there were no other people involved in this four-day-around-the-clock holiday, I felt left out. Burk's folks tried to include me, it wasn't that (I mean, they called me, "Daughter-in- Love" and stuffed my stocking to the brim for goodness sake), but it was still an undeniable "party of three" that none of the three of them could see they were having. On top of that, Burk had not been especially affectionate with me around his folks. And, while I wasn't expecting him to make out on the living room sofa with me like we were in eleventh grade, *some* affection that demonstrated he was in fact, in love, with me and we were soon to be married would have been nice. But instead, he was treating me like I was his cousin—not his bride. So that night after we got home from the day trip, it was late, probably around 10:30, I went and knocked on his door (that was literally 18 inches from my own) and said, "Hey can you come in here a for sec?" He said "sure" and came right over. And then *it* happened:

"So Burk, I'm feeling a little bit like you are...distant to me. Is my being here on your family holiday making you feel uncomfortable?" He scrunched up his forehead while half-closing one of his eyes and looked at me like I had two heads.

"Huh? What do you mean?"

"Burk, you haven't even kissed me since we got here. We're engaged. You shook off my hand at the Vanderbilt Mansion today when I tried to hold your hand. What is going on?"

"You think I'm supposed to act like I'm not at my parent's house??"

"Uuhh no—I think you should act like you're in love with me." I let it hang there. He was clearly either caught redhanded with his emotions of uncomfortableness as I suspected, or he wasn't in love with me. He got pissed.

"What are you accusing me of Robyn?! Are you accusing me of—"

"I'm not accusing you of anything Burk!" As I was getting a little more heated, "I'm just lonely. I'm away from my own family and my Dad is really sick and I'm feeling lonely and unloved. I need some reassurance..." Well, that was it: he was sufficiently mad now. He explained that he'd tried to give me a nice Christmas and he didn't think I was being grateful, which couldn't have been the furthest thing from the truth. I mean, he *had been* thoughtful. It was a nice Christmas. But he wasn't acting like himself and that made me feel strange. That's all I was saying.

Well, there was no explaining that to him. And like the momentary adolescent I had seen the day he came over to whine about Sheila's mission trip letter, he stormed out of my room and down the stairs where...much to my shock and dismay AND chagrin, his parents got involved. He had let them see how mad he was at me (and they couldn't "help themselves" but ask questions as they'd explained later on). It's a little fuzzy for me what came next, but all I remember is him sitting on the couch curling into a ball while whining and saying, "She won't let me love her!" His parents both stooped over him, Clark patting his back in a motion that said "there there" and his Mom tearing up. They were comforting their poor, poor son.

Yeh, I KNOW. That's what I said!

I seriously couldn't believe it. Where I come from (...my mom one of seven kids and my Dad one of six with six of his own children), NOBODY gets this much attention. Now before you all decide to hate Burk and his parents, the truth is this: Burk was such a pleaser back then that he could not hear this rational truth: "You are doing this one tiny thing that is hurting me in spite of the fact that you are also doing 999 things right." In Burk's mind, things were all good or all bad. My philosophy was different than that: mine is that a person's weaknesses can live side by side with all of a person's strengths. I don't think I knew until this moment, how far apart we were with our individual philosophies. But in that moment of me requesting a little more attention because I was feeling lonely, what he heard (which I did not say or feel for that matter) was "you suck."

And then well, he went to get reinforcements to prove to me he didn't suck, and it all just went down hill from there. Clark wouldn't listen to me. Viv wouldn't listen to me. Burk wouldn't listen to me. I felt like an outsider because I was an outsider. All I wanted was some affection from my FIANCE' during the last Christmas either of us would ever spend single (I don't know about you but it seems to me like the potential for a slightly romantic Christmas...) and not only did I not get that, I got pushed off their lily pad. They didn't mean to—it's just they never had to share it before in this way. None of the three of them were good at it yet. I finally said, "Ya know—I'm not conformable leaving this until tomorrow—could we perhaps talk about this? The four of us? The three of them looked at me incredulously, like... "Who does that? Who TALKS after a moment of family dysfunction?"

But I kind of insisted. The four of us sat down in the living room and before I could say anything, Viv had tears streaming down her face. Clark had already had one-too-many so he wasn't exactly helpful and Burk? Well Burk was staring into a plant on the coffee table. I was sitting on his left and he was saying things that were meant to be addressed to me...starting sentences that had the word "Robyn..." at the beginning of them, but instead of turning to talk to me, he was telling it to the green potted-succulent. I kept trying to explain that I didn't mean to ruin the day and that Burk, you're not yourself Babe, and that's all this was about, but he was so red-faced and angry, I could eventually tell that it was going NOWHERE!

So I went up to my room like an admonished 14-year-old and I have to say that if I'd known at all where I was geographically and it hadn't been this tiny town in the middle of nowhere, I would have left. Seriously, I would have gotten my purse, and hailed a taxi to the airport if I could have. I was angry and hurt, and still worried for my Dad without any affection from my man. Merry Effin' Christmas.

The next morning, I saw Clark first thing in the kitchen while getting his coffee and he said, "Now I don't want you worrying that we're 'thinking' anything. We don't hold grudges so don't sit around concerned about that, because around here we practice forgiveness." Here's what I wanted to say: "Thank you, you smug Jackass since you are the one who has poor boundaries and nursemaids your son through moments that should really have nothing to do with you and that you should have kept your nose out of!" and I meant that. If your grown, 31-year-old child comes running to you over a misunderstanding with his fiancé...in front of his fiancé?? Leave the room. Lock yourself in YOUR room. Don't get involved! Funny how I didn't feel like a daughter-in-love.

But I didn't say that to him. I smiled a reassuring thank-you smile and left it at that. But I was cool to Burk the remainder of the day and when we flew out at 6:00 pm, I'm not sure I've ever been more relieved to leave anywhere in my life. The truth of that saddened me. But I had just turned thirty-five, you know. I had a few moments invested in dreaming about this season of my life and how it would be perfect.

Just as I suspected however, Burk started acting like himself again in the air somewhere between Detroit and Grand Rapids and a day or so later, he was completely back. I still hadn't liked what happened—it did give me a red flag or two, but at least I felt assured that the problem was really between him and his parents, not between him and me. Burk was a grown up. Burk was a mature cool cat. He had a big important job and was trusted with a lot of responsibility professionally, but not unlike most of us, when he was around his parents he was reduced to a nine-year-old boy. Yeh it sucked, but we didn't live nearby them so we only had to put up with it once in a while, which is what I reasoned.

Twenty-five: The Beginning of Unlonely

Doesn't it seem like the title of this chapter should be "The End" since it comes near the end of the book? I guess a lot of people think weddings are an ending. But a wedding is the beginning! Burk and I got married on March 3, 2001. My Dad was too sick to be there though and actually passed away three weeks later, on March twenty-fourth. We didn't know how long he had left on our wedding day, though—only that he wouldn't be able to walk me down the isle. But ya know what? As sad as I was about that, I was committed to making the best of my long-awaited dreamt-for day. Unlike Christmas in Massachusetts, this time I wasn't going to attach an expectation of absolute perfection to it: instead, I decided to make it the best it could be under the circumstances.

And it was. Cole filled in for my Dad by walking me down the isle instead. Jeannine was able to successfully grow out her hair to a length that could be pinned up into an effective up-do and Lizzy managed not to have her baby during the ceremony. Decker was not only a more dignified dude these days, he'd married Paisley six months prior and was one of Burk's groomsman. The week before we had freezing rain and I began to freak out about the weather but Pastor Finn reminded me that if bad weather threatened to keep people away, I was still getting married, even if the only people there were him, me and Burk.

I knew he was right and that reassurance took the edge off. But guess what? It was a balmy fifty-five degrees and not a cloud in the sky. The sun was unmistakable, shining in my east-facing window when I woke up. And let me tell ya, after a Michigan winter? Fifty-five feels like the tropics around here. People put shorts on and lay out when it's fifty-five in March!

But what's even more interesting is that two days after the wedding we had a winter storm that was so bad, it canceled schools and knocked out power lines. So, freezing rain before our wedding day and a snow storm after: everyone got into town and everyone got of town, and our wedding day was gorgeous. It really did make it seem even more that it was meant to be.

Viv and Clark behaved themselves for the most part. We did have a scuttlebutt about where they were going to stay when they were in town for the wedding for the two weeks prior. They wanted to stay at Burk's but I said hell-freakin' no—behind their backs of course, not to their face. I said hell-freakin' no to Burk's face because I didn't want their boundary issues tainting the beginning of our life together. He agreed. So, they reluctantly stayed with his aunt who lived in Grand Rapids. And, they still called me their daughter-in-love, even after the ceremony, so they must not have been too mad about it. Oh yeh, and Viv wore beige. You know what they say about mother's of the groom and all: wear beige and shut up. So she was definitely growing on me.

And Burk? Well...Burk looked GQ-handsome in a tuxedo. After the ceremony, we ushered out our own guests instead of doing a receiving line at the reception. After the first couple of rows of guests trounced back up the aisle to the vestibule, the runner became cockeyed, running east and then back west again in a zig zag pattern. As we approached the third pew of waiting guests, Burk whispered into my ear, "Oh my gosh—That's a tort lawsuit just waiting to happen!" Between hugs and greetings, I asked Burk,

"Hey, do you *feel* married?"

"Not really: do you?"

"Not yet." I think I was expecting the fairy godmother to make an appearance and sprinkle magic fairy dust on us and suddenly we would levitate with the marriage feeling. I did know however, that I felt happy and unlonely.

Epilogue

A nd they lived ever after!

Notice I didn't say *Happily*—just ever after. This is good news! Burk and I have lived ever after, sometimes happily and sometimes not-so-happily and ya know what? If someone tells you that it isn't possible to live, or furthermore stay with their spouse whom they absolutely love, "unhappily" at times, it's not true. Burk and I are admittedly a high wire act. We're both feisty and strong-willed and well—let's face it, we were older to get married so we were both a tiny bit stuck in our ways. We both brought a Samsonite to our marriage, full of artifacts including old pains, disappointments, unreasonable expectations and some shame. (I mean, I KNEW going in that I had those things in *my* suitcase, but I was not expecting him to have those in his. It's a little arrogant to think that you're the only hot mess in the universe, huh?) We had some stuff to work through and we have. We still continue to work through stuff all the time.

But here's the good news—we still adore each other—we still, after 17 years of marriage in spite of the low lows, experience the height of the highs. And that's why we all need to hang tight. I submit that Happily-Ever-After redefined means, being able to stick it out with a Good Knight, and I emphatically declare I found mine. He was worth the wait and I believe this, whether we are in a season of happily ever-after or a not-so-happily ever after.

I think now that I've finished the book, Burk would say we are going into more of a happily-ever-after season!

However: I would like to say and am proud to do so that the same damn sign still hangs over my toilet to this day, even though I've moved five times since the little while colonial on Seventh Street. Hope has never left me.

Acknowledgments

I have so many to acknowledge for the great big contributions that have worked to inspire me for this project, but also those for the teeniest, tiniest little particles of inspiration that have also blessed this process. Those with large advocacies to this, my life's work, almost certainly already know who they are. But for example, one day when I was in the end stages of this project, I was feeling very discouraged because I had just received a call that my mom was back in the hospital for the umpteen-millionth time [six times in four weeks is a considered a lot, no?] Before I went up to the hospital to see her that day, I rushed to the store to grab some groceries to secure my household. I was in a fury, physically moving quickly and emotionally distracted, wondering how to take care of everybody, my mom, my nuclear family, my work, etc. While at the store, I ran into an old neighbor I'd rarely seen since I'd moved from the neighborhood six years before. She said, "Hey, how's your mom?" I answered by explaining she wasn't so good and was in the hospital again. Then she asked, "So then, how are *you*?"

"Well...you know....," I said, "...I'm okay, except for my guilt... I can't figure out how to be there for her and for everyone and everything else." I was becoming tearful. The neighbor put her hand on my shoulder and looked me in the eye and she said, "Robyn! You're such a good daughter!! You are doing a great job with everything." She smiled a knowing smile, the kind that feels like a hug. So, while I take a minute here to acknowledge inputs to this work, it is the simple moments like this one that endeavored me to finish it. It was the little encouragements from people about other situations having nothing to do with my work that gave life to my soul, and in turn, breathed energy into the literality of getting up every single day with intent and grinding out the capacity for it. If you know anything about writers, or are one, you also know there are a million reasons to never start a project like this. If by some miraculous process one actually has the courage to begin writing a book, there are then a BILLION reasons more, to quit it and *never* finish. So, thank you to God first, for bestowing me with simple moments of kindness, like the one with my neighbor at the grocery store.

Thank you to my beta-readers, Jerrod Nichols, Lori Van Hoef, Michelle Stoel and Staci Daniel, for your care and respect of this manuscript. Thank you for all you have given to it, to help shape it into the finished, glorious work it has become. Your input is the lifeblood of this work.

Thank you to Nanowrimo.org, for the challenge that inspired the original manuscript for this book in 2013.

Thank you to the published authors/editors that ever sat down and had a cup of coffee with me or ever invested in a long phone conversation, wrote me an email, or took the time in one way or another to encourage me with this work specifically, or in the art of writing Creative Non-Fiction. To Rhoda Janzen, David Staal, Anne Evans, Tim Evans, Elizabeth Trembley, Staci Daniel, John W. Phipps, Harvey Neil Stidson II, Jim Persoon and Glen Nishimura: this work would not exist without your inspiritment, teaching and in some cases, tough love.

To the work of authors who have influenced my work and my work *ethic*, I deeply thank Barbara Robinson, David Sedaris, Rhoda Janzen, Rick Reilly, Jane Austen, Frank McCourt, Erma Bombeck, Anne Lamott and Ree Drummond. Your work has taught me the delicate line that exists between satire/sarcasm, when it's balanced with truth. Too much "truth" isn't funny, while the best humor isn't funny without truth. Truth and humor need each other. As authors, you've managed the difficult task of finding the fragment of space in-between comedy and tragedy; you've figured out how to brilliantly dance on it, without discrediting either device. Not many can do this. Thank you.

Thank you to Julia LaPlaca, for some end-of-project line editing. [Walmart only one "l" and there are two t's in "Buffett." Duh!] This just goes to show why English teachers always say that when nearing a final draft, it's a good idea, at this point, to engage another pair of eyes.

Lastly, thank you to Carol Sonneveldt: if it weren't for your prayers and the hundreds of prayers you solicited on my behalf, I never would have found my Good Knight. And oh, to Clark and Viv: thank you for being good sports! I promise to redeem your characters in the sequel. Please love me anyway?!

I married a lawyer, right? So, I'm used to having disclaim things now. Yeh yeh, fine, so here we go. Ahem: most of the names and occupations have been changed to protect the guilty....and the innocent. In some cases, characters have been collapsed, as well as the use of literary devices incorporated, including but not limited to hyperbole, allusions, transferred epithets, and narration character- istics that frequently and intentionally change throughout. Creative Non-Fiction Memoir expects high integrity, that an author will "remember" to the best of one's abilities. But it also acknowledges that memories are tricky little buggers. It is common that another witness to the exact same scene may remember it a different way. Memoir suggests that both witnesses could be accurate in their accounts. [Don't worry—this used to make my head hurt too, but it doesn't anymore!] This work, although largely auto-biographical, falls into the genre of Creative Non-Fiction. To the best of my abilities, this is my story, creatively told.

Finally, a quick word to my local peeps and family: I really hope you enjoy this book. This work is really important to me, so I want to go on the record regarding the individuals for whom I wrote this book. It was not written in order to garner gossipy attention or hand-over-mouth dismay. On the contrary, this literary work was written for:

any person,

anywhere in the world,

whoever falsely believed

they weren't entitled to healthy relationships,

especially in the choosing of a spouse.

Addendum

My sweet Momma left this earth on February 18, 2018. At the time this occurred, I was in the eleventh hour with my publishing deadline for this book, reviewing the fourth, hardcopy prototype. Due to circumstances surrounding her passing and the months that followed, the project came to an abrupt halt for about six months. During this season, I deeply considered whether or not to change the areas in my book that refer to her in the present tense, to the past tense. I got to thinking though, about the discipline of Literary Criticism, an area of my profession in which I've spent a great deal of time, both writing and consuming. When writing criticism, analysts refer to the work of deceased authors in the present tense, because the work of that author, is currently, present to the analyst. In the spirit of this celebrated principle, I've decided to leave the references to my mother in the present tense. This is because she is present to me, but also [and mostly] because that's the way she would want it! Those who knew her are smiling right now;-)

"You own everything that happened to you. Tell your stories. If people wanted you to write more warmly about them, they should have behaved better."

—Anne Lamott

Made in the USA
Middletown, DE
19 December 2018